AF066150

Dr. Issam Wadi

THE LAST DROP
Humankind Post Oil & Gas

novum pro

www.novum-publishing.co.uk

All rights of distribution, including via film, radio, and television, photomechanical reproduction, audio storage media, electronic data storage media, and the reprinting of portions of text, are reserved.

Printed in the European Union on environmentally friendly, chlorine- and acid-free paper.

© 2018 novum publishing

ISBN 978-3-99064-115-6
Editing: BA (Hons) Rachel Jones
Cover photo: Dr. Issam Wadi
Cover design, layout & typesetting: novum publishing
Internal illustrations:
see bibliography p.131

The images provided by the author have been printed in the highest possible quality.

www.novum-publishing.co.uk

No part of this publication may be reproduced, stored in a retrieval system, or transmitted in any form or by any means, electronic, mechanical, photocopying, recording, scanning, or otherwise, except as permitted under Sections 107 and 108 of the 1976 United States Copyright Act.

This publication is designed to provide accurate and authoritative information in regard to the subject matter covered. It is sold with the understanding that the publisher is not engaged in rendering legal, accounting, or other professional services. If legal advice or other expert assistance is required, the services of a competent professional person should be sought.

All references used, where taken from the source, are to be used only in this book. If need be, please contact the reference and content owners directly for permission to use their content.

*To my lovely granddaughter, Dana,
to my other grandchildren and to the children of the world,
wishing them a safe and livable world when they grow up.*

CONTENTS

Preface	9
Acknowledgments	13
1.0 Introduction	15
2.0 Oil & Gas Today	18
3.0 The Illusive Golden Century	20
4.0 Future of Oil & Gas	26
5.0 Post Oil & Gas	29
5.1 Exploration and Production (E&P) Industries	30
5.2 Refining and Gas Processing	30
5.3 Petrochemical and Fertilizer Industries	32
5.4 Power Industry and Power Plants	32
5.5 Ground Transportation	34
5.6 Aviation	36
5.7 Shipping	38
5.8 Domestic and Home Fuels	39
5.9 Plastics	40
5.10 Electronics and Computer Systems	45
5.11 Home and Appliances	47
5.12 Textiles and Clothing	50
5.13 The Medical Sector	52
5.14 Steel and Aluminum	54
5.15 Wood and Logging	54
5.16 EPC and Mega Projects	55
5.17 Design and Engineering Services	57
5.18 Heavy Industry and Equipment	58
5.19 Coal as a Source of Energy	59
5.20 Renewable Energy	60
5.21 Nuclear Energy	61
5.22 Environmental Issues	62
5.23 Biofuels and Biopolymers	64
5.24 Urban Planning	65
5.25 Education and Research	66

    5.26 Petroleum Engineering 68
    5.27 The Food Industry 70
    5.28 Farming and Agriculture 73
    5.29 Sports 75
    5.30 The Space Industry 76
    5.31 Toys and Entertainment 77
    5.32 Tourism and Hospitality Industries 78
6.0 Global Impacts 80
    6.1 Impact on World Economies 80
    6.2 Impact on World Trade and the Financial Sectors 83
    6.3 Geopolitics 84
    6.4 Military and Arms 86
    6.5 Governments and Regulations 86
    6.6 Impact on Selected Business Sectors 88
    6.7 Social Impacts 96
7.0 Post Oil & Gas:
    Phases and Mitigation Planning 98
8.0 Let's Get Ready: The Way Forward 102
    8.1 High-Speed and Long-Haul Transportation 102
    8.2 Jet-Propulsion 104
    8.3 Electric Planes 104
    8.4 Miniature Nuclear Reactors 106
    8.5 Biopolymers 107
    8.6 Alternative Fuels 109
    8.7 Electronics and Computers 110
    8.8 Electrical Equipment, Cables, and Wires 112
    8.9 Battery Technology 115
    8.10 Farming and Agriculture Research 117
    8.11 Recycling 118
9.0 Summary and Conclusion 119
References 129
Index 131

PREFACE

It has been over a year since I started writing this book. It started in response to a question by my elder son, Walid, who asked me (when we were enjoying a sunny weekend at a nice resort at the Jumeriah Palm in Dubai),had I ever tried to study and analyze what is going to happen to the world when there is no more oil and gas? My answer was "No, never; at least not in a scientific and comprehensive way". The following week, after some initial research and analysis, I became attached to the topic, because I found out, for the first time in my life and after more than forty years in the oil and gas industry, that this question is more important and critical than I initially thought, and hence needed to be addressed properly. The more I researched the topic, the more involved I became in trying to find answers.

My work started by referring (at the time and until I sent the book for publishing) to the most recent and relevant research on the topic, whether by academia or by the energy sector, including the oil and gas industry. Although the consequences of oil and gas depletion were referred to in many relevant articles, research reports, and books, I realized that, apart from a few documentary films, general articles, etc., which were of a broad nature, there had not been a comprehensive, serious, nor in-depth study of the subject that addressed the impact or important aspects on our lives, nor discussed solutions and actions (i.e., mitigation plans) needed in a comprehensive way. Halfway through, I decided to convert this work into a book, finding myself obliged to tell the world what I found and what I thought. To be honest, the more analysis and research I did, the more worried I became.

My research revealed one and only one thing: "WE ARE NOT READY," and there are serious consequences waiting for us (not I or those of my age group, but waiting for our children and grandchildren). My worry level increased when I sent the first draft of the manuscript for proofreading by professionals and academicians, highly respected professionals, from different backgrounds and industries, such as those in in oil and gas, energy, technology, medical science, financial markets, and manufacturing. Furthermore, I was invited to speak about the topic at highly respected organizations and universities, such as the renowned Imperial College-London in UK and the University of Bradford in UK. In all these of interactions, my concerns were confirmed, since nobody could relieve my worries, nor could they challenge my pessimistic conclusions. Publishing this work is like sending an alert to the world, to wake-up, hoping it will trigger the right actions, based on global collaboration, looking for suitable solutions, so that the world can mitigate, if not all, at least some of the serious consequences that are going to face the world in a few decades.

One question I had to ask before I started writing this book was, "Who is my audience? Ordinary people? Specialized people? Academics? Business people? Who?" Due to the nature of the work, and given that this topic is of concern to every human and touches on most aspects of our lives, from simple things like toys, to complex entities such as the military, industries, politics, economies, technology, and so on, I decided to strike a balance and make it useful and readable by all. Having said that, there may be some acronyms and technical terms (I tried to minimize these as much as I could) that may be understood only by technical experts and specialists; however, you will still find that a vast percentage of the material is easily understood by the average person, and that everyone in his or her role in this world, field of work or specialty, will find most of the sections and material useful and relevant to him or her.

To make it easy to read, I have divided the book into 9 chapters (I refer to these as sections sometimes, they mean the same), that can be classified into three main parts: Part I, extending from Chapters 1.0 through Chapter 3.0, provide background, introductory information, and analysis that are related to the history of oil and gas development, the evolution and main characteristics of this industry. It also addresses the Peak Oil theory, including the work of M. K. Hubbert, the future of oil and gas, and the illusions faced by many nations caused by a flood of easy wealth in a short time, which many have assumed will never diminish and hence have used abusively.

The second part, starting from Chapter 4.0 and continuing through Chapters 5.0 and 6.0, represents the main material, all related to discussing the post oil and gas impacts on the world. Chapter 5.0 is the largest chapter in the book and address 32 areas and aspects of human life, from simple things like toys and furniture to major subjects like transportation, aviation, shipping, medical technology, and electronics. It analyses each one of these aspects and tries to explain, in simple terms, what is going to happen to these after oil and gas are gone. Chapter 6.0 addresses the post oil and gas impact, but on major professional areas, such as the economic, social, and geopolitical sectors.

The third part of the book, starting from Chapter 7.0 and continuing to Chapter 8.0, address areas related to the actions needed, alternatives foreseen, new technologies, and solutions that are promising as alternatives for some of the oil-based technologies, equipment, and commodities, such as the biopolymers, miniature atomic reactors, solar cars, etc. They also establish a high-level plan of action drafted to coincide with the oil-depletion curve, and the phases (as foreseen) that I propose. These are used as a basis to be followed by a more refined and detailed plan.

Chapter 9.0 addresses the effect on different businesses, presented in a tabular form, and explaining the respective impacts and severity levels for each. This chapter is a good reference for companies, governments, and investors, who need to know and foresee the predicted impacts, so that they can make the right decisions as early as possible and prepare for effects that transform businesses, replace products, and alter consumer practices. The section also shows if the solutions have concerns related to safety, security, or other possible consequences.

Whether you are a government official, businessperson, academic, industrialist, oil and gas professional, energy professional, investor, researcher, homemaker, student, soldier, medical doctor, contractor, manufacturer, military officer, or banker, I hope that you will find the book easily readable and useful, and that it will help you to prepare and contribute to your necessary plans and actions.

My last words: Let's save our children and grandchildren by ACTING NOW.

ACKNOWLEDGMENTS

It has been a year since I started researching and writing on this subject. The journey was not easy; bearing in mind my busy schedule, frequent travel, and family and social commitments. Eventually, the work was completed and ready to go. Without the help and support of many people, including family, friends, professional associates and academicians, this work could have not been done nor seen the light. Therefore, I want to thank all those who supported me while researching, writing, and completing it.

First of all, I would like to thank my son, Ghazi, for his great support. With all his busy schedule and job demands, he was instrumental in helping me, throughout, by reviewing the book material; helping with the diagrams, pictures, and graphs; and assisting in completing the references list. His support played major role in making this book happen. Also, thanks to my son, Walid, who motivated me to start this work when he asked me last year if I had ever thought about, or analyzed, what is going to happen to the world when there will be no more oil and gas. That was the starting point. Also, and as usual, with every journey or challenge I have been through in my life, thanks always to my beloved wife, Shahnaz, for her continuous support and encouragement. Similarly, thanks to my elder brother, Ghazi, who has been always a big motivator for me.

Many colleagues, friends, and professionals helped with the review and proofreading of the draft version; their comments were very useful, and both enriched and refined my work. I would like, in particular, to thank Mr. Marc Valleur, for his comprehensive review, discussions, and comments. Also thanks to Mr. Khaled Zayadin, Mr. Alan Stubbs, CEO, of Servelec Group-UK; and to Dr. Bernard Conseill, and Mr. Michel Buffenoir. Thanks also to Anita Balaji in NY, USA, for reviewing the parts related to financial markets and economies, and to Dr. Ghassan Hannoun for reviewing the parts related to the medical sector. Also, special thanks to Prof. Iqbal Mujtaba, Head of the Chemical Engineering Department at the University of Bradford University, for inviting me to talk about this book at the University, and to Mr. Neasan O'Neill, for inviting me to talk about this book at the Future Energy Centre of the Imperial College, London, UK. In addition, I would also like to thank Tony N. Al Saiegh for helping with the book cover design, Nabil Ayoubi for proposing the title, and Venita D'mello and Ron Bedua for extending necessary administrative and clerical support.

I cannot leave this page without thanking all those organizations and individuals who permitted the use of their important data, reports, material, graphs and charts; in particular I would like to thank Gail Tyerberg, Michael McDonald, and Paul Chefurka.

Thank you very much, everyone!

Issam Wadi
United Arab Emirates

January 2017

1.0 INTRODUCTION

Since its first commercial discovery in the 19th century, oil has been used as the main source of energy, and its production and consumption have increased exponentially, hence, it has become a dominant player in human development and growth. Today, it is used almost in every aspect of our lives, such as producing power, running machinery and factories, powering cars and other means of transportation, besides producing many different commodities that have become integral parts of our lives, such as plastics, clothing, and electronics. Without oil, our lives would stall.

Though many initiatives have been started in looking for alternative energy sources, in parallel with trying to find more sources of oil and gas, such as deep water and Arctic explorations, shale gas, shale oil, tar sand, etc. Many recent studies show that even if we are successful in producing more from these new and challenging sources, it is not foreseen that recoverable and commercially feasible oil and gas fuels will be affordable for more than a few more decades. As explained later in this book, it is obvious that the decline in the oil and gas production and reserve curves, has started, and are expected to commence in a steep downturn soon. In the past decade or so, many countries have started considering new sources of energy, such as renewable energy, as well as increasing their dependence on nuclear energy and using the remaining coal. Adding to this, the continuous growth in the world populations and the unprecedented economic growth in some countries (such as China and India), will accelerate the depletion rate of the world's remaining oil and gas reserves. It is foreseeable that some of the post-oil and gas challenges, can be handled adequately and smoothly by using new sources of energy, such as replacing gasoline- and diesel-driven cars by electric cars and replacing fossil-fuel power stations[1]

---

1 Fossil fuel power station: is a power station which burns fossil fuel such as coal, natural gas, or petroleum to produce electricity

by nuclear or renewable energy power stations. In the cases of aviation and shipping, the challenges are going to be harder and not easily resolved, due to the nature of the problem, especially for long-haul and heavy travel. Some of these applications will need decades of extensive research, supported by huge investments, to find suitable and viable alternatives. As discussed later in Chapter 5.0, there are many other post-oil and gas challenges that we are going to face, such as finding suitable replacements for plastics. Therefore, we urgently need to start looking for alternative commodities as considerable lead time will be needed to find and develop these to meet the huge volume involved. Some of these services and commodities are critical to the health, comfort, and safety of humanity. Without them, people are going to suffer, businesses will be affected adversely, factories will shut down, and our daily lives will slow down or stop. Examples of some of these commodities are plastics-based medical items and tools, computers, clothes, and mobile electronic devices, to mention but a few.

To add to the challenge, we should not ignore situations where oil and gas supplies are not enough or not feasibly available, which could lead to instability, eruptions of major wars, and political conflicts.. This book discusses, in its first few sections, the history and trends of the oil and gas industry since its early days, production and consumption patterns, and future trends. It then addresses the foreseen impact, caused by the absence of oil and gas, on almost every aspect of our lives, followed by a discussion of possible mitigation, plans, and solutions that need to be pursued to handle such impacts, in a humble attempt to avoid or reduce the foreseeable serious consequences. It also discusses alternative energy sources such as, biofuels (fuels produced from living matters), new transportation means and technology (the Hyperloop, rocket-like planes, electric vehicles), biopolymers; besides maximizing renewable energy production and usage. A large part of this book deals with the effect of oil and gas on the main aspects and needs of the world, such as social life, urban planning, world economies, education systems, technology development, medical systems, clothing and textile industries, military systems, and arms design, among others. The book also includes sections on the agriculture and food industries, and how these are affected by the absence of oil and gas, besides the impact of alternative energy sources, such as biofuel, on the availability of food, water, and the agricultural sector in general.

Although I have spent over forty years of my life in the oil and gas industry, thrived on it, learned from it, built my career and earned my living from it, I could not and will never claim that I have all the experience and knowledge, needed, to solve the foreseen huge problems after oil and gas, nor do I claim that have addressed all of the issues, problems, and challenges, although I tried. I spent months, researching all of the related areas and technologies, referred to the latest R&D worldwide, read many books on related subject matter and relevant reports, and held discussions with many experts from different backgrounds and countries, and still can't claim that I have covered everything, or that whatever I propose herein are the ultimate and only solutions. This is the best I could do in such limited time, and the floor is open for discussions, comments, suggestions, and further work by others. This is the beginning. The challenge is big, diversified, complex, and multi-fold; it therefore needs an army of scientists from over 50 disciplines and specialties, many research centers with enough funding for decades, so that we can all address it adequately, professionally, and successfully. Such research, to meet its objectives, needs to be supported by an international body with a global plan and collective effort by all countries, to ensure a smooth transition from an "Oil and Gas" dependent world to a "Non-Oil and Gas" dependent world. In a nutshell, the purpose of this book is to send an alert, create awareness, and invite the world to start planning, thinking, researching, and executing a collective and global plan as early as possible. Due to the complexity and size of the problem, if it is not handled probably, it is going to affect the lives of our children and grandchildren in a big way.

The most ironic thing of all is that after all these years of being heavily involved in managing, developing, and working in this great industry, in which I always have been proud to be one of its soldiers, now comes the time that I write about its death!!!

2.0 OIL & GAS TODAY

More than 60 years ago, geoscientist M. King Hubbert proposed his Peak Oil Theory. According to this theory, oil production would peak at one point and then start declining until its full depletion. As predicted by Hubbert's theory, we have started the decline already, and have only a few decades remaining until the world's oil is fully depleted.

British Petroleum (1) has estimated that the world has approximately 1.7 trillion barrels of proved oil and gas equivalent (equivalent refers to the energy value of each type of fuel, so can be compared or combined) in reserve. Shale oil, according to Energy Information Agency (2) studies, is estimated worldwide, as "technically recoverable" around 345 billion barrels; however this does not mean it will be "economically recoverable." Some studies challenge these optimistic estimates, and reports on United States shale oil have shown concern and doubt regarding these figures, although the cost of production of shale oil has come down significantly in the past few years, and technology is improving by the day. These estimates include the Canadian Oil Sands, estimated at over 160 billion barrels (3). The Arctic area is being targeted as well and explored actively.

One of the main challenges being faced by humanity is population growth, overuse of the planet's finite resources, and the dumping of waste, which makes it hard for our environment to accommodate. The answer today, as concluded by Paul Chefurka (4), is "sustainability"; he describes a "sustainable population" as "one that can survive over the long term (thousands to tens of thousands of years), without either running out of resources or damaging its environmental niche (in our case, the planet) in the process". He has added that this means that our numbers and level of activity must not generate more waste than the natural processes can return to the biosphere, so the wastes we do generate do not harm the biosphere, and that most of the resources we use are either renewable through natural processes or are entirely recycled if they are not renewable. Paul Chefurka has developed models for population growth, and has concluded that that the current population is not sustainable. He also concluded that with the decline of oil, which is an important supporter of what is called the "carrying capacity" and since oil will be depleted in a few decades, then a population decline is inevitable. His model shows that a sustainable population will need to be 1 billion in 75 years, which is a big challenge to achieve based on a decline in birth rate.

Many studies have shown a strong correlation between the world Gross Domestic Product and consumption of energy, which explains the strong contribution of oil to the world's "activity level", hence its impact on the "carrying capacity" of the earth.

3.0 THE ILLUSIVE GOLDEN CENTURY

I would call the century following the 1940's when oil started to become an essential commodity in our lives, not only as an important source of energy but also as the foundation for many other essential items used by us every day "the illusive golden century." The entire world enjoyed the new energy source, consumed it with little or no caution or wisdom, whatsoever; in fact, over-relied on it. This commodity was abused in a way that caused damage to the environment, contributed to an exponential increase in population beyond the "carrying capacity" of the environment, as stated by Paul Chefurka (4), plus made many oil producing countries fully dependent on it for their development and growth; furthermore, it made many of them "high-income economies." Many of these countries, though enjoying the benefits and revenues from oil and gas production for decades, have provided a high standard of living for their people with little or no real industrial or technological development, and so have not benefited from this highly unsustainable revenue to build a robust and productive economy that is based on industrial knowledge, technological development, and equitable social conditions that can be sustained and used in a post oil and gas era. This phenomenon is very visible and obvious in many third world countries, hence the recent downturn of the oil industry has brought huge negative impacts on most of them. People in these countries, to a large extent, have lived the "illusion of oil and gas"; become dependent, complacent, and less or even non-productive, assuming that such natural wealth will last forever, and hence are never prepared for the "post oil and gas" era. I do not think that human beings have lived such hugely illusive experiences like this, or pursued such lavish lifestyles, since the start of human civilization thousands of years ago. The approach to this precious and valuable gift from god (which needed tens of millions of years to evolve and be transformed into oil),.has been highly short-sighted, causing harm to earth and making many nations fully dependent upon it. Our children and grandchildren will be the victims of our irresponsibility, negligence, and short-sightedness. A good example of countries who started so early, preparing for this inevitable destiny is United Arab Emirates (UAE), who started diversifying its economy some years ago, so its economy is less dependent on oil. In fact, the leadership in UAE said last year; "UAE shall celebrate the day when the last oil barrel is shipped from UAE". Fossil fuels (refers to all types of fuels produced from earth such as oil, gas and coal) contributed extensively to the second and third industrial revolutions; today we are not sure whether the speed and acceleration with which that happened was the optimum or best for humanity. That is yet to see. I believe that the fast development of the world economy, by large, was driven by the greed of companies and businesses, who created the consuming society, which was consuming energy, commodities, and other relevant services without justification. As per most analysis, the world has consumed roughly double of what it really needed of energy and relevant commodities. This, in turn, has reduced by half the time available for this resource on earth, which will forbid future generations from benefiting by it, as well as give humanity time to prepare for alternative sources and means.

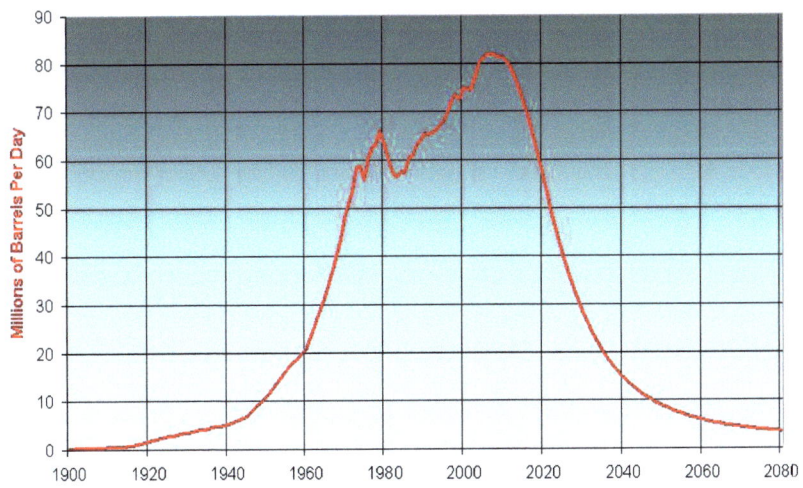

Figure 1.0 – shows oil production since started and until its end (4)

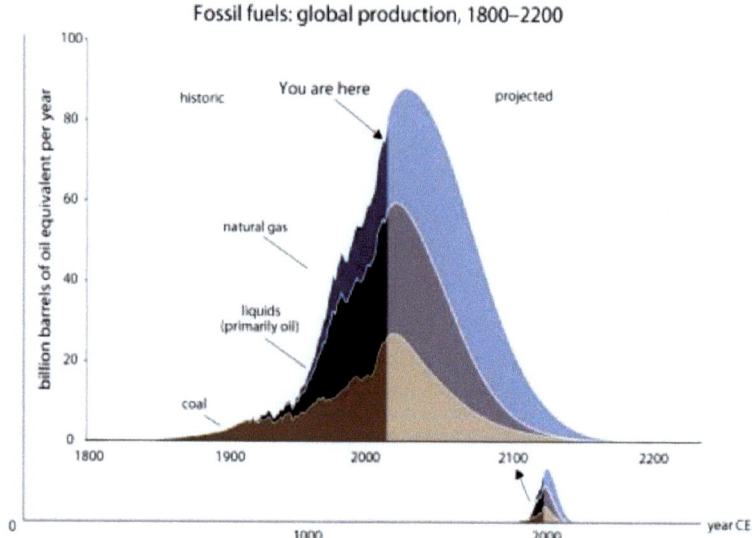

Figure 2.0 – (courtesy of Rocky Mountains Institute-USA) shows global fossil fuel production since the mid-1800s and forecast until it is exhausted (5).

Figure 2.0 above presents the actual figures and forecast of global fossil fuels in barrels equivalent, for the period from the year 1800 to the year 2200. We started consuming fossil fuels in the last half of the 19th century, however our consumption started to rise exponentially by the mid 60's of last century, as seen in the curve above. This curve predicts that the fossil fuel peak (not oil and gas alone) is happening in the next 1–2 decades, while as per other estimates, like those of M. King Hubbert (6), the oil peak has passed already. In best estimates, the decline in fossil fuels will start soon. Adding to this, coal is not always a suitable fuel to be used to replace crude oil and gas in many applications and usages, such as aviation, cars, etc. Not to mention the impact on our environment. Also, producing gas or oil from coal is not always easy or economically feasible. Furthermore, major parts of the existing reserves are not easily or economically recoverable, which makes the situation worse.

As discussed previously, in the 50's of the last century, Hubbert expected that the oil production curve would take the form of a bell shaped curve, as shown in Figure 3.0 and Figure 4.0.

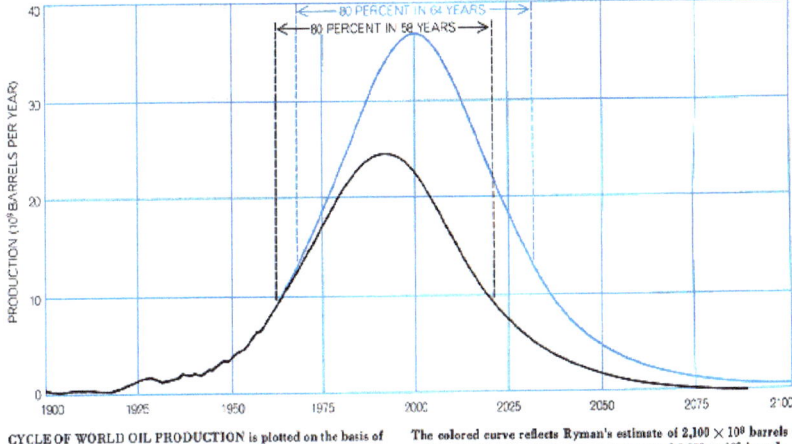

Figure 3.0 – Shows the Peak Oil Production (two estimates (6).

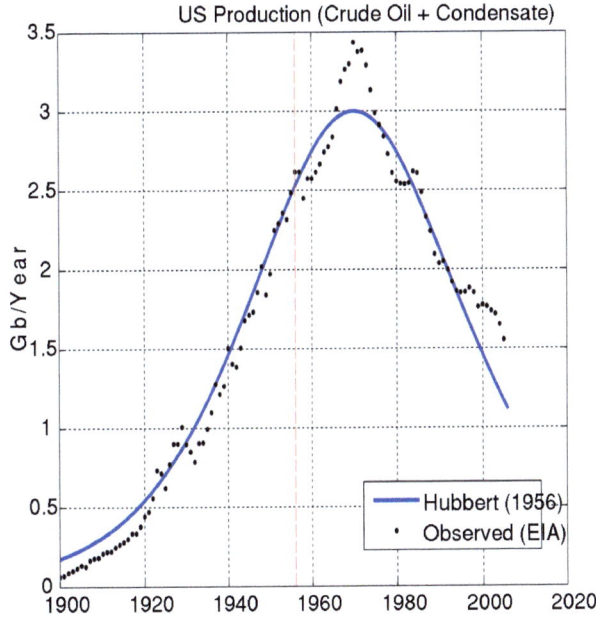

Figure 4.0 – U.S. Oil Production and M.K Hubbert's prediction (7)

Hubbert, in his analysis more than 60 years ago, predicted that American oil production would peak in the 1970s. Furthermore, he used the same method to predict the peak in global oil production. He estimated that global oil would peak in the mid-1990s, which he later adjusted after the 1973 oil crisis by shifting the peak by 10 to 15 years. According to analyses done later, Hubbert's estimates were relatively accurate when compared to the actual oil production.

Figure 5.0, below shows human population growth against oil production between the year 1000 and the year 2010. It shows that human population has started to rise exponentially along with the rise of oil production. I believe the increase in population was triggered initially by the discoveries and massive usage of coal, which started earlier than oil in the 19th century.

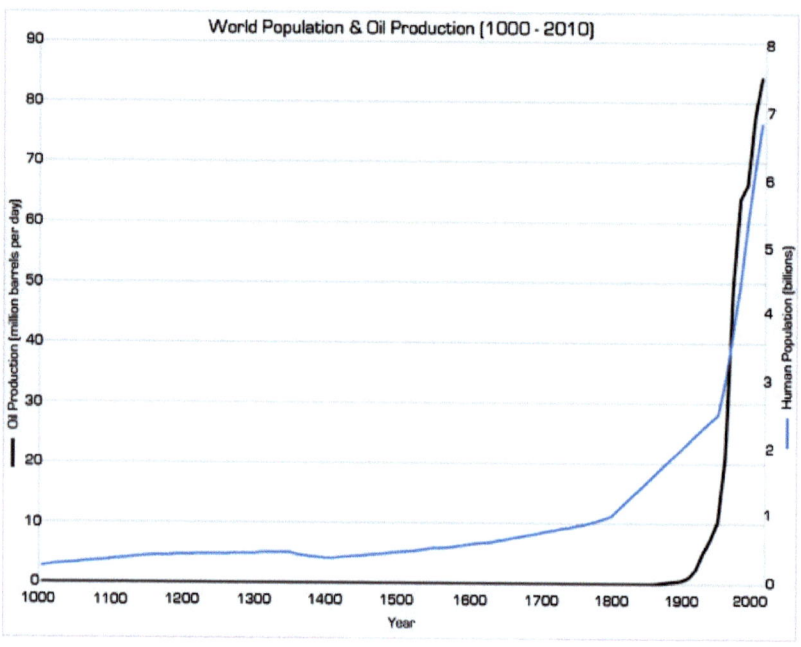

Figure 5.0 – World Population and Oil Production 1000–2010(8)

According to British Petroleum statistics of 2016 (1), the world has about 6600 trillion Standard Cubic Feet of reserve gas, which are estimated to last for about 52 years.

In gas studies, analysis, predictions, and production, one of the big challenges is recoverability, which can be as low as 35%. Also, the gas quality can be an issue. Based on my forty years of experience in the oil and gas business, no matter what reservoir modelling and simulation tools companies use, or how much experience they have, there is always some kind of uncertainties, surprises, and unpredictable results in gas reservoirs and fields, either related to depletion rates compared to estimates, gas quality unexpectedly changes in some cases (e.g., the gas turns extremely sour after certain period of production), or recoverability becomes too difficult and/or too costly. Furthermore, there are always challenges with gas re-injection[2] to enhance oil recovery; this, in turn, can reduce available gas for production.

As to the shale gas story in the USA, there has been extensive work done by Berman (24) using mathematical models for thousands of wells in the Barnett, Fayetteville, and Haynesville shales. He has concluded that operators have significantly exaggerated their claims, and he has added that reserves appear to be overstated by more than 100 percent. He has added that, "typically, the core 10 to 15 percent of the shale formation's gas is commercially viable. The rest may or may not be." Berman, using his model, estimates that production falls steeply for the first 10 to 15 months, followed by a weekly hyperbolic decline.

---

2 gas re-injection: is the reinjection of gas into an underground reservoir, to maintain the pressure in the reservoir.

4.0 FUTURE OF OIL & GAS

Tom Paine, the English-American activist and philosopher who lived in the 18th century and considered one of the founding fathers of the United States, wrote some of the most influential pamphlets of the American Revolution. He said, "If there must be trouble, let it be in my day, that my child may have peace."

    Since the discovery of oil, the world has consumed over one trillion barrels, while the confirmed remaining reserves are estimated at more than a trillion barrels. With the economic growth in some countries, driven by population growth, industrialization, poor discipline, and the culture of most people that live on this globe, the world is expected, by most estimates, to consume the balance of its reserves in a few decades; however if we take the optimistic view of things, add new discoveries of unconventional oil and gas, consider enhanced gas production, and add to this the remaining recoverable coal, then, at best, one may assume fossil fuels, at current and foreseeable consumption rates, will be enough for probably another 50 to 70 years. This estimate takes in consideration continuous growth in building renewable energy sources (which are exponentially accelerating in growth, especially the solar energy-based ones), additional nuclear energy plants, plus minor increases in the use of biofuels (which are still limited in most countries), so the current consumption of fossil fuels can be maintained at current rates, or at best will be reduced over the coming few decades. If we take the best scenario into consideration, economically recoverable fossil fuels are expected to converge to zero, before the end of this century which is not that far away. If we take the worst scenario which is what I believe in, this commodity will be gone much earlier than the end of the century. Such times will be lived and seen by our grandchildren and probably by our children.

    Figure 6.0 (9) and Figure 7.0 (10) show the world energy consumption by type,.It is obvious that fossil fuels are still the main source of energy, compared to biofuels or nuclear. Coal is still a major source of energy in the world. Renewable energy (especially solar energy) is ramping up sharply, which is another exponential pattern that hopefully will counteract the exponential decline in fossil fuel production. This alone, as will be explained later in this book, though important for humanity, is not enough to handle all the challenges caused by the absence of oil and gas.

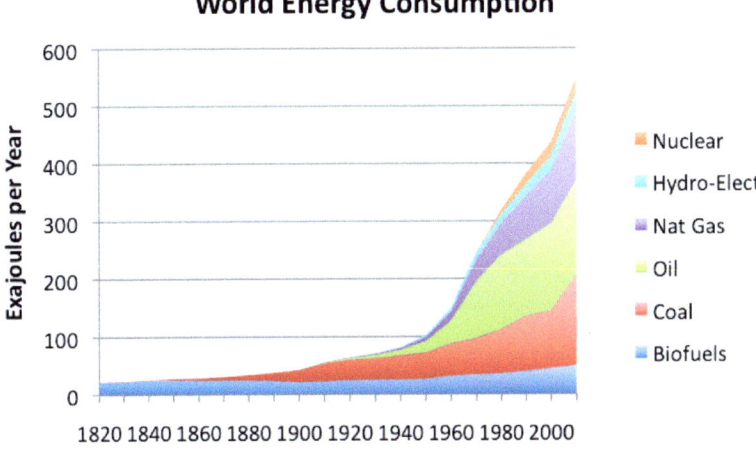

Figure 6.0 – shows world energy consumption by type since the early 19th century (9).

Today, fossil fuels and hydrocarbon products are not only used as a fuel source, whether at homes, factories, and farming, and for use in automotive and aviation applications; they are also used to produce other important products that we have become so dependent upon, like plastics, sulfur, ammonia, and urea. These are important commodities for human development, helping to produce food, furniture, supporting health services, the computer industry, construction, the military, and many other major human activities. These products have become essential parts of our lives, as they are used in critical applications and services. As the famous chemist Dimitri Mendeleev noted in 1892, oil must not be burned, but must be used exclusively for organic synthesis.

As per Figure 6.0, fossil fuels are still a major source of energy in the world, and form over 80% of the energy sources used today. Figure

7.0 shows the different sources of energy, whereby it is obvious that renewable and nuclear energy are the fastest growing, compared to fossil fuels.

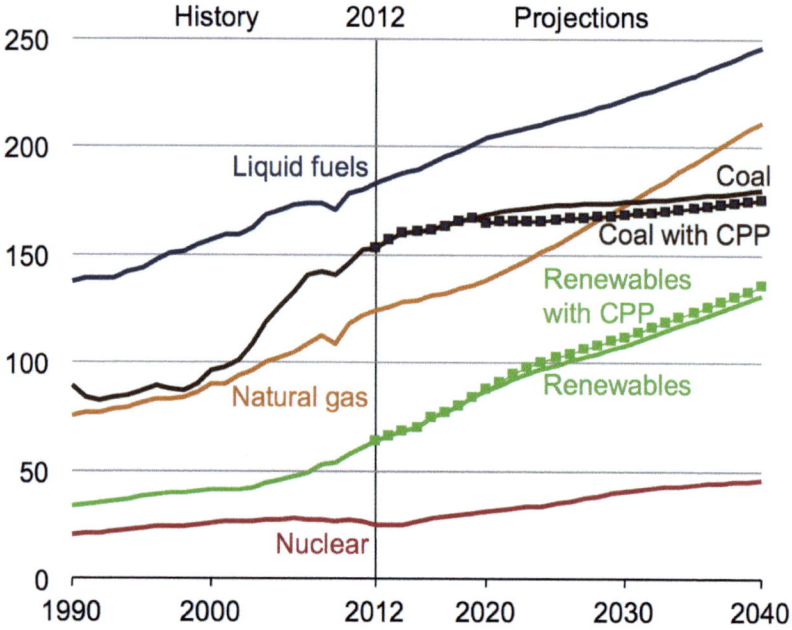

Figure 7.0 – Courtesy of EIA/Theenergycollective.com website, International Energy Outlook-2013(10)

The above figure shows how fossil fuel energy is declining vs. renewable energy, which is rising.

Most of the remaining oil and gas reserves will be in the Middle East and Latin America. According to BP (1), by the end of 2015. Saudi Arabia has one the largest remaining reserves, which is around 266.6 billion barrels, followed by Iran, which has around 157.8 billion barrels, followed by Iraq with approximately 143.1 billion barrels, and Kuwait with 101.5 billion. The United Arab Emirates have about 97.8 billion barrels.

5.0 POST OIL & GAS

The following sections discuss the "post oil and gas" phase, its impact on the different aspects of human life, and how the absence of this important resource will affect humanity in almost everything that we do, use or need. As I will explain later in this book, some of these impacts are critical and serious; in fact, in some cases they may become catastrophic, unless we prepare for a reasonable alternative, ready and usable by the time oil and gas resources start their last and steepest descent to complete absence from our lives. As explained earlier, at the best and by the most optimistic estimates, this steep decline will start in one or two decades at most, which by all standards is a short period for us to be prepared and ready, bearing in mind that some of these alternative sources or means need extensive research, preparation, and development, supported by an international collective and global collaboration. The world needs, at first, one global strategy and plan to prepare for the "post oil and gas" era. Though some initiatives have started already, like the renewable-energy development and deployment, like biofuels and research and development of new means of transportation, these are not, in my opinion, adequately developed to replace all of the current "fossil fuel" produced energy and commodities. Similarly, in the case of new transportation means and technologies (e.g., Hyperloop, rocket-like planes, etc.) that are being explored to replace some of the current, conventional, long-haul means of travel, they are not expected to be ready by the time fossil fuels are fully phased out. Furthermore, many of these alternatives, even if proven technically successful, will need to be proven economically.

5.1 Exploration and Production (E&P) Industries

The exploration and production industries rely fully on the presence and usage of oil and gas. With the diminishing of these same resources, this industry will be hit badly. Although some of the tools, knowledge, and technologies used in this industry can be employed in other industries and for other needs (e.g., drilling, geology-related services, reservoir engineering, etc.), and so may serve other fields that will survive the post oil and gas crisis, such as water exploration or mining, we may foresee that such requirements, though important, will not be enough to consume and employ all the E&P resources and capabilities that have been developed over many decades, employ millions of people, and utilize expensive assets, worth hundreds of billions of dollars. Hence, we expect that the E&P industry will shrink greatly and will become a minor player in the new "post oil and gas" energy era. The sector will need to transform its business model in a major way and re-salvage some of its expensive resources, so can maintain some continuity at the time.

5.2 Refining and Gas Processing

Oil refining and gas processing industries are called, in oil and gas terminology, "downstream" industries, in analogy to the upstream industry, which covers the oil and gas production fields. These industries are based on major and complex processes; that were developed more than 100 years ago. They constitute a cornerstone in the oil and gas industry. This sector has become more critical for the world, as it generates important products that are used extensively by people, industries, businesses, and the military. Examples of these dependencies are:

- fuel for cars, buses, and trucks
- fuel for ships
- fuel for aviation
- plastics for home appliances
- plastics for computers and electronic devices
- feedstock to produce a range of chemicals, petrochemicals, and fertilizers
- domestic fuels
- fuel for farming and agricultural equipment
- fuel for military needs
- fuel for construction equipment and machinery

Can you imagine in a few decades that this important industry will almost vanish or shrink substantially, limited to processing scarce and expensive fuels or used to produce small quantities of biofuels, or produce fuels from processing remaining coal? Even if we assume that the world will discover new sources of hydrocarbons (hydrocarbon refers to oil and gas fuels and products) from new sources like algae, or other possible sources, I expect that these will be limited, expensive, and insufficient.

Having said that, the industry will not vanish all of a sudden, and there will be a transition phase, during which the world will need to phase out this fossil fuels, while focusing on producing fuels that will be needed for critical human requirements, even for short periods, and until feasible alternatives are found (e.g., aviation fuels, shipping fuels, etc.). While the world should look for alternatives in different areas and for different needs, developing things like biofuels, biopolymers, solar energy, nuclear energy, etc., we will need to change the current design of refineries and gas plants, so as to maximize the production of critically needed products, such as aviation fuel, diesel fuel for agricultural equipment, heavy fuel oil for ships, and so on, during this transition phase.

We may also need to maximize the Gas to Liquid (GTL) plants and processes, so that we can produce liquids from the remaining gas sources, assuming that gas sources will last slightly longer than crude oil sources.

5.3 Petrochemical and Fertilizer Industries

The petrochemical and fertilizer industries are also dependent on oil and gas products, used as feedstock for their plants, such as ethane, propane, and naphtha. In the absence of these products, the petrochemical and fertilizer industries can't operate. This leads to the loss of important products that we need, such as plastics, urea, sulfur and ammonia. To face this situation, we need in place the right mitigation measures, plans, and actions. Examples of these are:
- Start Rationalizing the production, hence the usage of plastics and limit it to essential needs only.
- Maximizing and improving recycling of plastics, as discussed later in section 8.11.
- Increasing the production and development of biofuels and biopolymers, in a balanced way, as explained later in sections 8.5 and 8.6 so as to meet the essential needs for fuel and plastics without harming the ecosystem and food production.
- Finding alternatives, such as using natural fertilizer products, or finding new manufactured ones that are affordable and suitable.
- Developing crops and plants that need less fertilizer, to grow and produce.

5.4 Power Industry and Power Plants

Since it started in the 19th century, the power industry has been a cornerstone of the industrial revolution and of human development. From early days, power plants were either coal-based or hydropower-based. Later on, with the discovery of oil and gas, the power industry started shifting to these new fuels, using them as the main source of energy for producing electrical power. Examples of these fuels are natural gas, diesel fuel, petroleum distillates, and heavy fuel oil. Coal has remained an important source of energy for many power plants worldwide, while in some countries it is the main source. A decade ago, renewable energy started to be used as a source of electricity at the commercial level; however, it still represents a small fraction of the world's total produced power (less than 10%), while hydrocarbon-based fuels represent about 50%, and coal about 26%, (refer to Figure 7.0, above). The world energy is trending towards an increase in building and using renewable energy sources versus fossil fuels (refers to all types of natural fuels produced from earth, such as oil, gas and coal). However, the forecast that renewable energy will trend exponentially so as to cater for the foreseen exponential decline in fossil fuels, combined with a continuous increase in the world's population, makes this race vital for the humanity, given its impact on our lives, especially if we are not ready by the time oil and gas are gone. In the past decade or so, we started seeing more and more countries targeting and starting renewable energy plants, as well as building power plants based on coal and nuclear energy. Today the world consumes about 21 billion Megawatt Hours (MWH) of electrical power, which is expected to increase by about 2.5–3% each year. It is foreseen that this will continue even during the transition phase (i.e., the last two decades before oil and gas are gone). However, as stated earlier, most of the generated power in the world by that time will be renewable. Some of this energy will be integrated, connected to the national power grids, while some may continue to be isolated and local. Nuclear power plants will continue to be built, and at higher rates than they are now. Coal-based plants will also be used for a few more decades after oil is finished, especially in countries producing and having this commodity, due to the high cost of shipping at that time.

5.5 Ground Transportation

Today, most transportation means use of some kind of hydrocarbon fuel to run cars, taxis, buses, ships, or trucks. The majority of these use either gasoline or diesel fuel. In the past decade or so, many countries have started converting public transportation and taxis to more environment friendly fuels or energy systems, such as liquefied petroleum gas (LPG), compressed natural gas (CNG), solar, electric, and hybrid. Many countries also have started giving incentives to people to use electric and hybrid cars which are increasing in sales and are becoming popular throughout the world, although they still represent a tiny percentage of the overall number of vehicles in use in the world today. The world produces approximately 4 million hybrid/electric cars of all types. If we assume there are about one billion cars worldwide today, then these hybrid and electric vehicles represent about 0.4% of the overall number of cars. This is a tiny fraction; however, with the fast rate of increase at which these cars are produced, their percentage of the overall number of vehicles is expected to be significant in few decades, which is GOOD NEWS under the foreseeable diminishing of hydrocarbon fuels.

In some countries, biofuel pumps have been installed at fuel stations, although only a small percentage of vehicles use them, e.g., mostly in the USA and Brazil. With the current and expected trends in switching to alternative energy sources and fuels, we do not expect that a full replacement can be achieved within five to six decades unless a highly accelerated plan is devised and followed. I estimate that by 2060, 75–85% the world vehicles at most will be electric, small percentage run on biofuel or other type of energy. The challenges being faced to replace all nonrenewable hydrocarbon-based fuels in transportation can be summarized in the following:
- Adequate and fast development of alternative energy sources, for cars, such as electric cars, hydrogen-fuel cell cars, biofuel cars, and hybrid cars, which are commercially and technically feasible. Other challenges that will face the transportation industry, especially road transport, such as buses, cars, trucks, and the

like, is finding suitable material to make tires, bearing in mind that today this relies heavily on oil and gas products, assuming that natural rubber and neoprene will not be enough to meet world demands at the time. Furthermore, there will be the challenge of finding replacement for asphalt and bitumen, which together is the main product for building roads. It is needless to talk about grease and lubricants, which are needed by most machinery, equipment, and vehicles.
- Limitations in the battery technologies and the need for more and accelerated R&D to improve their power density and reduce re-charge times.
- Cost of using biofuels, as compared to conventional fuel beside its huge impact on production of food.

Ground-based transportation, with all the challenges described above, are the least affected, as per my analysis, compared to airborne and seaborne transportation systems.

The current trends and technology development in electric vehicles, supported by new habits, discipline, and ways of living (like relying more on public transportation, more localized societies, etc.) should create an acceptable basis for a new era with regard to land transportation, even if we do not rely heavily on biofuel-based vehicles. In the cases of shipping and aviation, there will be limited feasible alternative sources of energy and fuels, like biofuels, due to limited availability and impact on ecosystems. Furthermore, usage of electric engines and solar energy in limited cases (mostly short-haul travel on small ships and planes in countries where there is adequate infrastructure for charging their batteries) will not provide a full and adequate solution for all aviation and shipping needs, especially in cases of heavy long-haul travel. Estimating that aviation alone, will be consuming, after 50 years, using current growth trends, more than 15–20 million barrels of fuel per annum (which is very difficult to produce from biofuels), we therefore foresee that the world will save the then valuable biofuel that will be critical to aviation, shipping, and other critical needs such as medical, security and fire-fighting cars and equipment. Any surplus (I doubt there will be any) may be used for other critical transportation means, such as ambulances and police cars. It also will be controversial if such scarce and valuable fuel will be spared for military usage, bearing in mind the need for survival challenges that humanity is going to face at that time. The discussion above has assumed that electric-driven transportation will be maximized, as much as possible, so as to reduce the demands on biofuels, especially for land transportation, and wherever electric and solar solutions are technically and commercially feasible (e.g., trains, metros and light railways, cars, buses, power plants, etc.).

5.6 Aviation

Aviation is probably going to be the most serious and challenging sector when hydrocarbon fuels are not available any more. Aviation fuels depend largely on kerosene, which is one of the refined products of crude oil. Its technical name is aviation turbine kerosene (ATK). Kerosene in different grades and forms represents a large portion of fuels used by people today. Kerosene is also used in some countries as a domestic fuel; however, this is not a major challenge compared to kerosene needed for the aviation industry.

Due to the nature and criticality of the aviation industry, it is not foreseen that there will be an alternative fuel, which is technically and commercially feasible, to replace ATK. Several countries have experimented with new types of fuel for aviation, such as biofuels, which are feasible technically to replace current aviation fuels; however, these are not expected to be available in large quantities to meet all aviation fuel requirements, and they expected to be more expensive. Solar energy also is being tested, but again, it is not foreseen to be feasible for large planes, or for long-haul and loaded flights. Nuclear energy is not going to be feasible due to cost, security, and safety reasons, although there has been some early research and concepts being examined in that field. There are over 300,000 commercial, cargo, private, and chartered flights every day all over the globe. The world consumes a huge amount of aviation fuel; about 5 million barrels of jet fuel per day, which is about 6–7% of total oil consumption. In my opinion, trying to promote biofuels as an alternative fuel, whether for environmental reasons, which is the main motive today by many countries and U.N. organizations, or due to preparation for the post oil and gas era, should be done with a long-term plan, wisely and carefully, due to its impacts on other critical industries, such as food and possible impact on the earth's ecosystems. Setting the right priorities for the usage of biofuels is required while considering the following:

- The criticality of biofuels for the aviation and shipping industries, post oil and gas, due to the reasons explained above with respect to the lack of feasible alternative sources of energy for these two industries, especially for long-haul and loaded travel. Hence, these two industries have priority, compared to cars, trains, and buses, unless other new long-haul transportation means (e.g., Hyperloop) are developed and made technically and commercially feasible within the coming two to three decades.

- Another option, which may be developed and might be feasible with time, is the miniature nuclear reactor, which is being researched by a few countries, such as the USA, UK, Russia, and China. If found technically feasible for planes, it will still remain to be proven and justified commercially, as well as safe and secure. As per the article of Michael McDonald (11) in OilPrice.Com of July, 23, 2015, Boeing has recently patented a nuclear-powered airplane engine. The engine uses laser "combustion" and, if it could be effectively implemented, the system would allow a plane to travel, literally, for years without stopping. Of course, pilots would need a break periodically, and so it's more likely that the technology would be combined with a drone-style pilot. From a military perspective, this would be an enormous advancement. Having stated that, I still believe that such technology may be feasible only in limited military and civilian aviation applications, such as huge civilian and military planes and ships.

- The other option for the aviation industry is to explore the feasibility of electric-powered propelled engines, combined with supplementary solar power. Whether this can be justified for large planes and for long-haul travel has yet to be explored. Such a solution also needs the right infrastructure and technology developed to charge the batteries that it will use. There are technologies being researched using some kind of laser beams to charge the batteries remotely from ground stations (may install the laser charge transmitters at current ground-aviation stations along aviation routes), supported by some solar energy that is not foreseen at present to be enough to provide continuous and sufficient power for heavy and long flights, and hence it is expected to provide a supplementary role only.
- Electric planes and solar planes are foreseen to play important roles for smaller, short-haul and light planes. Planes using rocket-like fuels, such as hydrogen, oxygen or a mix are not yet technically developed, and so it is too soon to examine their techno-commercial feasibility. I foresee that these will not be adequate to support large and heavy planes, beside other safety issues, associated with the production, storage, transportation and usage of hydrogen. However, these alternatives are worth further investigations and research.

5.7 Shipping

Approximately 90% of world trade is carried by the shipping industry, using over 50,000 ships transporting all kinds of cargo. Without shipping, world trade, import and export of goods, will stall.

The shipping industry is another industry that will be affected significantly post oil and gas. Almost every modern ship, vessel, yacht, small or large boat uses some kind of hydrocarbon fuel. Having said that, small boats and ships that are used for entertainment, fishing, heritage display or some kind of sports may still be using wind power or human muscle to sail. A few large military ships and submarines use nuclear power. Therefore, ships that depend on fossil fuels, such as diesel or heavy fuel oil, represent a very large percentage of ships used worldwide (close to 100% for merchant ships). It will not be easy to find alternative fuel for such ships in the post oil and gas era. Biofuels are technically feasible; however, at the scale and volume foreseen, the cost of biofuels, besides the limited quantities of biofuels available, are not going to make it feasible to switch all merchant ships to biofuel. Hence, I foresee that the shipping industry, like aviation, will be hit badly if we do not find an alternative that is both technically and commercially viable. This means that the world trade and economy will be affected tremendously. Electric engines, combined with solar energy and some kind of sails, may be workable in the case of small ships, ferries, and boats travelling for short distances and between locations and ports that are equipped with battery-charging systems. However, the same will not be achievable for large boats, ships or vessels. We may be going back to the "steam engine times," with ships driven by coal; and though this may be technically feasible, it still will rely on a diminishing fuel. Not to mention, the environmental impact – namely the difficulties associated with coal. Beside biofuels, there may be a need to develop some kind of miniature nuclear-based engines for large vessels, as have been proven and tested for military ships for several decades.

5.8 Domestic and Home Fuels

Domestic fuels are used at homes, farms, and small businesses, depending on different oil and gas products, such as kerosene, fuel oil, diesel fuel, liquefied petroleum gas (LPG), and propane. Most of the time, these are used for heating, running generators, pumps, boilers and at times for producing local electricity. A small percentage of people have started using renewable energy, such as solar and wind, to meet part or all of their energy needs, which vary from one country to another. For example, countries like the USA, Canada, India, Jordan, the European nations, and China have started earlier than others in using renewable energy systems, ranging from wind turbines, solar farms down to simple solar systems to heat water. Considering the nature of domestic energy requirements, this is not going to be critical during the post oil and gas phase, because renewable energy costs are going down and renewable energy lends itself perfectly to domestic energy usage. Locally produced electricity may or may not be connected to the national or local grids, depending on the country and respective regulations and incentives. Hence, we do not see huge concerns with respect to domestic and home energy needs.

5.9 Plastics

Inorganic Chemistry Frontiers

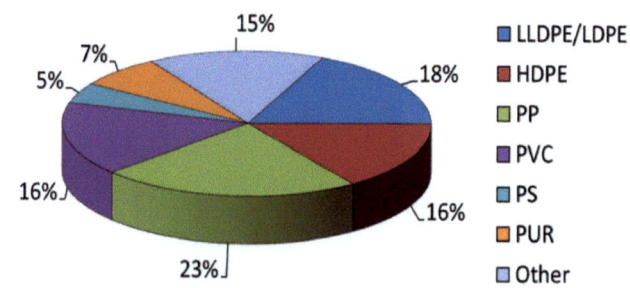

Chart 1 **2012 World polymer demand.**

Figure 8.0 – The world's plastics production by type (12)

Since the 60's of the 20th century, the world production of plastics of all types has risen to reach over 320 million tons. Plastics production and usage is increasing annually by about 5%. In the past few decades, plastics have replaced at a very fast pace many materials that were used by people for many centuries, such as wood, cotton, glass and metals. It is worth mentioning that plastics-producing facilities and factories consume over 8–9% of the world's oil and gas: half of it as feedstock to these factories, and the other half as energy.

Figure 9.0 – Example of plastic commodities and items used by us every day.

Plastics are used all around the world, almost in every aspect of our lives. They are of different types and specifications; however, all are produced from hydrocarbon fuels, such as methane, ethane, and naphtha. Plastics are used at home, office, factories; in cars, trucks, airplanes, mobile phones, TVs, computers, military equipment, and countless other items which have become essential parts of our day to day activities and needs. Today, it seems impossible to live without plastics. Sixty years ago, people did not use plastics, rather they used wood, paper, metals, glass, leather, textiles, etc. to satisfy their basic needs, such as producing shoes, sandals, cooking pans, utensils, toys, clothes, car interiors, furniture, and other items. With the boom in oil and gas, followed by that in the petrochemical industry, we became so dependent on plastics, that it became extremely difficult to do without them. Such dependency was driven, to a greater extent, by the versatility and economics of plastics, compared to other products such as glass, wood, and paper. This will probably be one of the most serious post oil and gas challenges that the world is going to face. If we try to categorize the impacts on the world when there are no more synthetic plastics, and are trying to put our priorities right while preparing for that phase. I would rank these impacts as follows:

- Critical applications and needs that have major impact on our lives, health, safety, and/or incur big costs if they are going to be replaced (e.g., medical equipment and items, manmade fibers (clothing and textiles), food packaging, crops-cover sheets, farming plastic greenhouses, insulation for electric cables and wires, electric breakers and switches, electronic items, computers, mobile phones, airplane external materials (composites) and internal items).
- Important but not critical; needed for convenience, plus make commercial sense (e.g., automotive interior materials and decorative items, upholstery, tubing and fittings, manmade fibers used for curtains, carpets, pens, stationery, etc.)
- Nice to have but if missing, we can still manage with minimal impact (e.g., large water and fuel pipes, furniture items, kitchenware, utensils, tiles, decoration items, building material, etc.)

To reduce the impact of post oil and gas with respect to plastics, the world needs to research and develop alternatives, as well as introduce new cultures and regulations, such as:

- With immediate effect, we need to maximize the storage of spent plastics and off spec plastics (off spec plastics are plastics that are rejected by plastics producers and sold in bulk to smaller factories, to produce general and lower quality products), so that the same can be recycled when the world production of plastics is diminishing. This may have some environmental impacts if not done properly, hence the need for regulation and proper management, plus the development of the right solution for storage of these plastics for long times and recycling of them when they are needed. This step will provide the world with more time to find suitable post oil and gas solutions. If we assume that we waste and dump about 5% of the world's plastics yearly (I estimate it is much more), this is equivalent to over 15–20 million tons per year. Saving this quantity for the coming, say, 50 years, means we will have over 750 to 1000 million tons of saved plastics, which can serve the world for a decade or so, assuming that it will be used only for essential needs at the time.

- Consider using alternative materials, such as aluminum, brass, wood, and leather (depending on the application). These alternatives need to be examined carefully in light of cost, available reserves, energy needed to produce them, impact on environment, and suitability.
- Start introducing, expanding, and developing applications based on biopolymers for essential needs, (e.g., medical items, electronic boards, and essential electric items).
- Change current engineering practices and manufacturing standards, while building and executing new projects, producing equipment, cars, ships, and planes, by using alternative methods, designs, and materials, which will avoid or reduce using plastics as much as possible (e.g., overhead power-lines rather than buried power-lines; paper-insulated windings rather than plastics; paper-oil insulated cables (like it was a long time ago); reduce the usage of HDPE (high-density polyethylene) and other plastic-based pipes; use metal-based fittings such as copper, steel, and stainless steel). Use wood, aluminum, or other metals for doors and windows, as well as for internal items in cars and planes.

Figure 10.0 – Plastic-based pipes, used to transport water, fuels, and other liquids.

Figure 11.0 – Example of cables and wires using PVC, which is one type of plastic.

5.10 Electronics and Computer Systems

The electronics and computer industry depends heavily on plastics to design, build, and produce different components and items. In the absence of plastics, this industry will face major challenges, as plastics are used to build important parts of these systems, such as the casings of computers and electronic equipment. Plastics are also an important component used in building internal parts, such as printed circuit boards (PCBs), master computer boards, electronic components, ribbon cables, internal wiring, etc. Though it may be argued that casings can be reasonably replaced by glass or metal-based products, like aluminum, there will be challenges when it comes to electronic components and wiring, which depend heavily on plastics to manufacture and build. To deal with the challenges, foreseen post oil and gas when plastics will be scarce, following are some proposed ideas and suggestions which may be considered and need further research and development:

- Continue to research and develop new computer and electronics technology that are less dependent on plastics or use fewer plastics to produce the same function, such as biochemical computers, biomechanical computers, optical computers, and quantum computers. Although these are still in their infancy stage of development, worth exploring.
- Use biopolymers in a very cautious and rationale way, and only as needed, due to their cost and scarcity at the time.
- Maximize recycling of plastics, use these for building computers and electronic devices with caution, like biopolymers, due to the scarcity of plastics at the time.
- Extend the useful life of these devices, including computers, laptops, mobile devices, and servers, so instead of replacing them every 2 to 3 years, extend their usage to a cycle of 5 to 10 years (although this may face the greed of suppliers, who push for high turnover of these devices, to generate more revenue and profits; the issue has to be regulated and controlled, due to its serious impact on the world). One may argue that such policy may adversely affect human development and progress, due to

the limitation imposed by using older hardware. Our argument is that applications, software functions, and features produce the main improvements and enhancements needed by users; it is not the hardware. Though we may need to sacrifice some unnecessary functions, due to hardware limitations, I believe that with a new approach to designing operating systems and software (SW) applications, which should be more efficient, and focus on essential functions and needs, we can capture most of the functions of what we get under the current regime of high turnover, upgrades, and short replacement cycles of systems, while still using a ten-years-old hardware. Furthermore, suppliers need to optimize what is provided on these machines and make it more tailored to specific needs, and so reduce the unnecessary burden on the hardware, by removing unessential SW functions and features that are not important for every user, based on the concept of "fit for need" (FFN).

- Semiconductor manufactures should try to find new materials to replace plastics in their design, and/or find alternative ways to build boards, such as replacing cables and wires with printed copper buses and replacing plastic covers and parts with ceramics and glass.

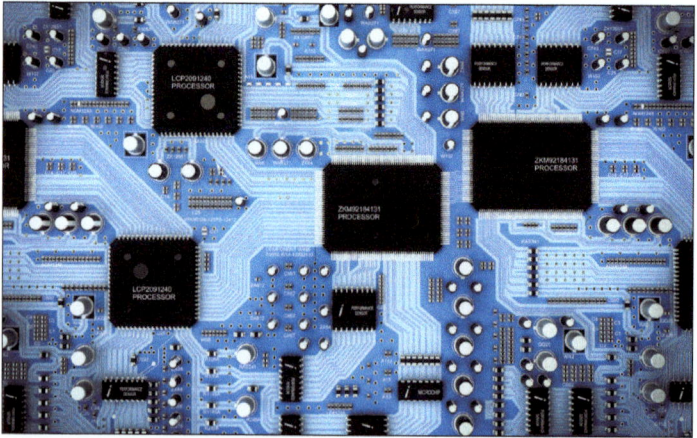

Figure 12.0 – Example of a printed circuit board (PCB).

5.11 Home and Appliances

One of the main impacts on the post oil and gas world will be the absence of plastic or plastic-based household products used extensively by people. Almost every appliance, tool, piece of equipment, or house item we use today is made of or has some kind of plastic component. Examples of these are furniture, kitchenware, carpets, windows, doors, toys, hoses, cups, trays, tools, and many others. From today's perspective, biopolymers are the only technically viable source of plastics. Unfortunately, this alternative has two drawbacks: it is expensive and it is difficult to produce in large quantities. Biopolymers are produced from biomass, which like biofuels needs land and water. This is going to be an issue in a few decades due to competition with food demands. Biopolymers may be produced and used only to make items for critical and essential applications, such as medical instruments and components, electronics, food preservation and packaging, etc. Post oil and gas plastics will become a scarce commodity and luxury item that will not easily be affordable. Many of today's simple, cheap, and affordable plastic items used on daily basis by almost every one of us will not be readily available at that time. Most of these will need to be replaced by other materials, such as wood, leather, aluminum, tin, steel, glass, silver, and nickel.

Figure 13.0 – Shows evolutions of sandals and boots. On the left, wood based sandals, used pre "oil and gas boom" and on the right, plastic ones, which are used by people today.

Today, most homes use conventional power, coming from the national or local grids, or in limited cases, individuals using isolated sources of renewable energy, such as wind or solar power at homes, either to supply all their needs. In some countries, people have been using solar energy to heat water for the past five decades or so. Some projects have started to help people who live in isolated, rural or remote areas in Asia and Africa to produce energy using wind turbines and solar energy to meet their basic energy needs. Good examples of these are projects supported and built recently by United Arab Emirates (UAE) for several countries in Asia and Africa. Another impact for us at homes will be related to the sources and types of energy and power we use. Most homes foreseeably will have one of the following power sources, or some combination of them:

- Locally produced power from simple solar and or wind sources, installed at each home. These may or may not be connected to the national or local grid, depending on the country, location, and regulations.
- Central power coming from the conventional power grid, either as the main source of power or as backup (in which case solar or wind energy is the main source).
- District central solar or wind power, supplying towns and cities.
- Use of wood or coal for some or all of home heating requirements.

Some of the challenges that will face us at that time will be to find replacements for refrigeration gases used in refrigerators, freezers and air conditioning (HVAC) chillers. The same applies to commercial applications as well.

Most, if not all buildings and homes, will use some kind of built-in solar panels on the building sides, roof or external surfaces to produce energy. Backup batteries may be used to store energy for the "no-sun" days or during nights, unless other sources are available for backup, such as grid power. Most homes will grow their own vegetables and fruits, using local farms, backyards, gardens, even small balconies and roofs. They will use modern technologies, which help in growing plants, with little or no soil. Homes will use smart energy management systems to conserve and save energy. Due to the maximized usage of public transportation, parking spaces either will not exist at most homes or will be minimal. Home design will maximize natural ventilation, improve water usage, rely on energy management systems, beside wastewater recycling and treatment systems.

Furniture will resort back to wood (also, it will be constrained due to deforestation concerns and issues), textiles, and leather, as it used to be decades ago, combined with some aluminum (limited due to energy concerns) and steel used in furniture. Kitchenware will use wood in utensils. Doors and windows will rely more on wood instead of plastics. Curtains and carpets will not use plastics any more, but will rely on natural fibers, as were used a long time ago. Similarly, tiles will not include polymer components. Most home appliances, such as refrigerators, washing machines, dryers, irons, tables, TV sets, and vacuum cleaners will be built with little or no plastics. Things like hoses, handles, casings will be made from alternative materials such as wood, aluminum, steel, glass, and nickel. One of the other challenges to be faced while building homes and offices will be to find suitable replacement for insulation, water proofing, and sealing materials that are not dependent on oil and gas.

To conserve land, more-high rise buildings will be used, so land can be spared to produce food.

Figure 14.0 – House with built-in solar energy panels on its roof.

5.12 Textiles and Clothing

Since the oil and gas boom a few decades ago, the trend of producing and using hydrocarbon-based fibers (or manmade fiber) versus natural fibers, like wool and cotton, has been increasing. The former has been increasing exponentially since the 1980's, while usage of natural fibers like cotton has increased at a lower rate, and wool has remained at an almost steady rate. Cotton- and wool-based textiles and clothes were dominant in human life a few decades ago, while today they form a smaller percentage, compared to manmade fibers (combined, they form fewer than 30% of the total useable fibers). The ratio of natural fibers to manmade fibers will continue to decrease further, driven by the lower cost of manmade fiber, less land available for growing cotton, and the boom in the plastics industry. The manmade fiber production is taking an exponential growth pattern, like many other oil-related products, which is not a good sign, knowing that it will start declining in only a few decades, driven by the decline in the oil and gas industry, besides the limited land available for growing natural fibers and the huge increase in world population that has occurred since oil was discovered.

The other side of the story is that the textile and clothing industries depend on fossil fuels in their production processes, both for operating the farming equipment and in the making of clothes and textiles.

If we assume that renewable energy, such as solar and wind, beside the public grid power, will be available for respective farms and textile factories, then the main challenge will be producing enough natural fibers to replace manmade fibers. This means, using the current ratio of manmade fibers to natural fibers, that we will need to produce 4 to 5 times the current volume of natural fibers, which is going to be a huge challenge, bearing in mind the limited land available, food requirements, and scarcity of water at the time.

If we use the current basis, it is expected that manmade fibers will represent over 75% of the fiber used in the next 4 to 5 decades, when the oil and gas is phased out. This will make the situation very challenging. It took over 6 to 7 decades for plastics to overtake cotton and

wool, hence it might take longer to reverse the curve again, bearing in mind that this will need, beside new regulations, incentives, and enough land and water to increase the production of biofuels (so as to use some of it to produce biopolymers), and so on. What can help during this phase are some changes in our habits and cultures like:
- rationale usage of clothes with reduced consuming culture;
- maximize recycling of fibers of all kinds.

Failing to do this will render humans to look like their ancestors during the Stone Age.

Figure 15.0 – What we will look like if we do not find adequate solutions for post oil and gas shortages in fiber.

5.13 The Medical Sector

The medical sector is one of the most critical and important areas for humanity, due to its impact on people's health and wellbeing. This sector will be affected heavily, post oil and gas, in different aspects and areas, starting from important medical items and tools that are dependent on oil and gas components, such as plastics (e.g., disposable items, such as syringes, gloves, etc.,) to drugs and medicines, which need components such as sulfur to produce them. However, tools such as surgical tools, dentistry tools, and others will be minimally affected. Medical furniture, like beds, chairs, desks, closets, and sheets, will need to evolve to products that use minimal plastics.

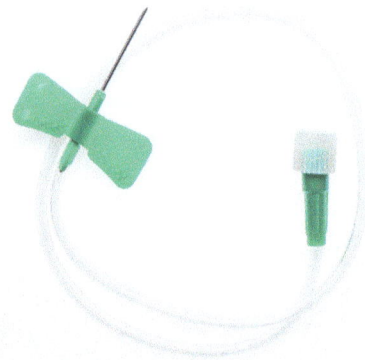

Figure 16.0 – The catheter, which is a critical medical item that is dependent on plastics. (Courtesy of www.123rf.com)

Regarding power supplies to clinics and hospitals, like homes, will depend on a mix of different types and sources of energy. However, in the case of hospitals, a power backup arrangement will be a must, using uninterruptable power supply (UPS) systems and/or backup diesel generators (based on biofuel).

It is expected that in the post oil and gas era, medical needs and the types and severity of illnesses will change, caused by the major change in life styles, aging (thanks to the oil boom), other environmental aspects, and allergies caused by related oil- and gas products. Today, pollution and illnesses caused by exposure to chemicals, oil-related gases and fumes are high, and may cause cancer, allergies, asthma, and other illnesses. The reduced use of oil and gas will have a positive effect on some of these illnesses. However, the increased usage of metal-based products, post oil and gas, is expected to result in an increase in other types of illnesses, such as skin-related allergies (e.g., eczema). The decrease in use of plastic-based items at home, such as curtains, bed sheets, and carpets, and the replacing of these by wool, cotton, feathers and other natural fibers is likely to cause an increase in allergies (e.g., asthma, sinus allergies, etc.) related to these substances. We can expect that the number of car accidents will fall, in light of the reduced need for travel in private cars, along with the increased usage of public transportation. Due to the foreseen reduction in the ability to travel, especially for long, across the ocean distances, there may be less of a spread of infections and epidemics, although the limitations in travel may affect adversely the world's ability to deliver medicine and medical services to other poorer countries.

One of the main concerns, which is difficult to analyze, predict or put solutions to, will be the impact of unbalance in the earth's ecosystem, for example, in case people start removing forests for food or biofuels. The same will have long term impact on many things in our lives, including our health.

In summary, and due to the importance of this sector, we believe it will be given the highest priority when it will come to distributing and providing energy or using scarce resources, such as recycled industrial plastics or biopolymers.

5.14 Steel and Aluminum

Steel and aluminum have been used by humans for many centuries. With the first, second and third industrial revolutions, the usage of these have increased exponentially. Also with the development in structural engineering, design tools, and capabilities in manufacturing of automobiles, planes, and ships, the usage of these materials has increased rapidly. In fact, in several areas and applications, they have become a good replacement for wood, concrete, and other materials. Aluminum was discovered around the mid-19th century. Today, the world produces over 9,500,000 tons of alumina. Though post oil and gas quantities of this material and of steel alloys used in the oil and gas industry will decrease substantially (e.g., building oil and gas plants, oil and gas wells, production platforms, gas processing plants, pipelines), there will be new requirements for these commodities, driven by new power plants, biofuel plants, huge infrastructure projects, and new means of transportation, which will need large amounts of steel. We see increased usage of aluminum (though high energy will be needed for production), mainly to replace plastic-based products in buildings, cars, and furniture. Overall, we do not see big or serious impact in this sector, post oil and gas.

5.15 Wood and Logging

Ever since humans have existed on this earth, wood has been, and remains one of, the most important products used by people for different applications and needs. These include: arms, heating, homes, carts, farming equipment and household items. Today wood is still an important product used by people for items such as furniture, heating for remote and rural locations and many new practices such as decorations, tiles and art. A few decades ago, with the oil and gas boom, some of wood's applications started to be replaced by new material produced from oil and gas, such as plastics. Examples of these are home accessories and utensils, construction materials (doors and window frames), kitchenware, etc.

Wood was also the main material used to build homes, to build ships and boats, and to build planes' and cars' interiors. In the past decades, these were (depending on the application) replaced by other materials: steel, concrete, aluminum, and plastics. With the diminishing of oil and gas, it is foreseen that wood will resurface again, to take its position again in our lives. Today, there are several successful attempts to build high rise buildings using wood. Some people may also resort again to wood for heating; hence logging will increase as the cost of other sources of energy may rise substantially. Wood will also come back to build and decorate cars, as it used to be in the early days of automobiles, due to the high cost of post oil and gas plastics. I foresee also an increased demand for pulp & paper (P&P) to replace plastic sheets used for packaging, plastic bags, and plastic sheets for farming. The main challenge, in this case, would be the impact on our ecosystem and the competition for land and water against production of food needed for human consumption (and animals of course), at that time.

5.16 EPC and Mega Projects

The oil and gas sector is one of the main clients of mega projects. Mega projects, or as called at times EPC projects (Engineering, Procurement, and Construction), is the classification of projects done usually on lump-sum basis. Some people call smaller lump-sum projects EPC projects; however, in this book, I want to differentiate and limit this classification to those large and costly projects of over a billion dollars' value. Other areas that also use mega-projects are the power sector, water sector, mining, shipping, aviation, aerospace, chemical, and infrastructure sector, besides the military and government. In this book, we will focus on industrial mega projects, as our discussion is related to oil and gas.

Most oil and gas mega projects are complex and expensive (in some cases, a single project may cost in excess of 20 billion dollars). The oil and gas mega projects are needed, for example, to build green field oil refineries or expand existing oil refineries, gas plants, petrochemical plants, and develop or expand existing oil and gas fields. In the post oil and gas phase, most mega projects will not be needed in this sector; they may decline with the decline of the industry. In the power sector, though nuclear-based projects will continue to exist, and most of these are huge in value, renewable energy projects will increase in number; however, most of them will be smaller in value compared to oil and gas projects. The infrastructure sector will continue to grow, especially for connecting lands (to substitute for sea and air travel). Some of these will be huge and complex. Large aviation and ship building projects will be fewer. Similarly, chemical and petrochemical projects, which depend on oil and gas, will disappear or be much fewer in number than today (they may be built for biofuels). Furthermore, and due to the involved project logistics, many of these projects will be built by local contractors, with fewer international and foreign contractors involved. Because of the difficult logistics and the tendency to become self-sufficient, most countries will maximize the use of local resources, material, and equipment. Movement of large numbers of people and equipment to remote locations will be difficult and expensive at that time. Having said that, remote and offshore engineering and design services will still be done by international and foreign companies. The new situation will affect the development of some third-world countries, which have limited local resources (people, equipment, technology, know-how). A century ago, when people moved to another country to work, it meant they migrated to that country and, most likely, they did not come back to their home country again. So, when a country brought thousands of people to help on a local project, these people most likely came to settle and did not go back home again, due to travel costs and financial difficulties. We expect that the same may happen again post oil and gas. This will have an impact on respective population structures, immigration laws, and movements of people.

5.17 Design and Engineering Services

In the post oil and gas phase, it is expected that there will be a major impact on engineering and design standards and practice, as a large number of these standards organizations like the API (American Petroleum Institute), ASME (American Society of Mechanical Engineers), and ASTM (American Society for Testing & Materials) were developed on the back of the oil and gas industry. Though some of these standards are already updated to cover renewable energy systems and industries, as well as biofuels processes and plants, they are still in need of major reform to remove irrelevant parts, add new sections and standards, and update existing ones as needed. The new design, engineering practice, and new standards will also emphasize new requirements to meet the post oil and gas challenges in a more effective way, such as:

- More focus on biofuel products and systems.
- Deal with new materials needed to replace plastics.
- More emphasis on energy conservation, especially in plants and equipment using the remaining hydrocarbon-based fuels in the transition phase, before these are totally depleted.
- With the accelerated depletion of some existing reservoirs, there is the possibility for these to turn into sour fields, hence there is a need for special care in the design and material, so that the same can be exploited, safely and effectively, until their final depletion, which may extend to a few decades.
- Update the design of planes, ships, and vehicles to suit the new technologies, material and sources of energy.

- Design electric equipment and systems to suit the new constraints, such as the absence or reduced availability of plastics, besides the distributed nature of power plants (renewable mainly). Hence, we foresee more usage of overhead power lines, and resorting to ceramic, glass, paper, and other non-plastic insulating materials. Also, expect to resort to paper-oil insulated cables, transformers, and motors, as was the case seventy years ago.
- Develop efficient engines that consume less energy.
- Develop new designs for miniature nuclear-energy power engines and plants, to be used standalone for trains, planes, and ships.
- Modify oil refineries in the interim to produce high value and scarce but needed products, such as naphtha and kerosene. We will also need to maximize gas to liquid (GTL) plants and processes, so we can produce liquids from remaining gas sources, assuming that gas sources will last longer than oil sources (some studies show that gas may last 40–50 years after oil).

5.18 Heavy Industry and Equipment

Heavy industry deals with producing large, complex, and important equipment, machinery or tools, such as cranes, excavators, ships, vessels, industrial equipment, gas turbines, steam turbines, pressure vessels, tanks, heaters, boilers, and the like. Heavy equipment are of three main types: static, rotating or mobile. Many of these such as cranes, shovels, huge motors, compressors, turbines, heaters, and boilers, need some kind of energy or fuel to function. Most static (or stationery) equipment needs energy to perform mostly as a source of heating, such as distillation towers, boilers, reactors, and tanks; this can be provided from sources such as solar energy.

In the post oil and gas phase, equipment which need energy or fuel to perform, such as gasoline and diesel, will, considering the scarcity of biofuels at the time, be expected to be built using electric motors, solar, or hybrid engines. However, there might be cases where biofuel may still be justified.

5.19 Coal as a Source of Energy

Coal was one of the first fossil fuel sources, used by people since the early days of the 19th century. Initially, coal was used for domestic purposes, such as heating and cooking, besides producing steam to drive large ships and trains. Later it was used to produce electrical power by means of steam turbines.

Coal was gradually replaced by oil and gas, starting from the early days of the last century. However, coal still represents a large percentage of the electrical power produced today in the world; at over 40%, as per the World Bank estimate (worldbank.org-tables 3.7, World Development Indicators) (13). According to BP (1), the estimated world reserves of coal are expected to last for about 114 years, based on the current proven recoverable reserves of coal worldwide. Due to environmental issues, many countries have started replacing coal with hydrocarbon fuels and nuclear energy since the 1960's; however, in the past decade or so, and due to high prices of oil and gas, many countries have started looking at coal again as a viable source of energy. It is expected that the world will continue to rely more and more on coal and maximize its usage in the coming 40–50 years, and will depend on it more in the post oil and gas era to meet some of its needs, given that it is estimated to last a few decades after oil and gas. It is foreseen that in the interim phase, more plants will be built to produce liquids and gas from coal, so coal can substitute for some of the missed hydrocarbon fuels, post oil and gas.

5.20 Renewable Energy

Renewable energy is growing aggressively worldwide. In fact, many countries are aiming to produce over 20% or more of their energy needs, using renewable energy sources, within one decade or so. A few countries have already achieved this target. It is foreseen that this will continue until a major part of the needed energy is produced by renewable sources. Renewable energy can be used for producing power, whether in isolated areas or integrated with the national grid. Also, in transportation, such as cars and buses, solar energy may prove feasible when combined with electrical energy using batteries. Solar and wind energy have proven to be viable and reliable sources of power, especially with the significant reduction in building and production costs. These are now competitive with even the lowest-cost energy sources, such as gas-driven power plants, especially when solar energy is produced on a massive and national level in an integrated way. We have seen projects with costs per KWH (kilowatt hour) as low as 5 to 7 cents, and in some recent projects, down to 3 cents.

There remains the challenge of providing energy for planes and ships, where, as discussed in previous sections, there will be limitations and constraints in the practical use of renewable energy. As explained, renewable energy may be used in limited cases (e.g., supplementary to electric engines in certain cases, like short-haul travel, small and light planes, small ships, etc., combined with other sources of power, such as batteries), but these will not provide full replacement and alternatives. Therefore, renewable energy will be emphasized wherever it has proven itself, both technically and commercially, so as to produce electricity, or produce heat that can produce steam. Similarly, electric vehicles, combined with solar energy, have been proven as well, and will be further improved and extended, whether in electric models or as hybrids. The world will target for replacement any existing fossil-fuel energy sources, using renewable energy besides nuclear energy. There are studies in the USA to produce hydrogen from renewable energy, such as wind and solar, which may be used as fuel in future planes, rockets, cars, and probably in fuel cells. It is worth saying that there are still major challenges (e.g., issues related to energy storage, maintenance of the solar cells, recharge time of batteries, power density of batteries) that need solutions on a priority basis for solar energy to dominate in different sectors. Also, countries with low solar energy yield indices and limited sunny times will be less favorable when it comes to producing and using solar-based solutions.

5.21 Nuclear Energy

Nuclear energy was developed and used, starting in the 1950's, by major countries like the UK, France, the USA and Russia. Other countries, such as China, followed suit in the 60's. This technology was used, besides potential military applications, to produce power, including powering large military ships and submarines. Having said that, it is worth mentioning that the usage of nuclear power has gone through a cyclic pattern, varying from one country to another. Some countries have started decreasing the number of their nuclear power plants, like Germany, while others are steady users, such as France. Several countries are increasing their nuclear-based energy, such as India, UAE, Jordan, and Egypt. Today, nuclear energy represents slightly over 10% of the total electrical energy produced worldwide. Seeing the trend in different countries in building nuclear power stations over the past few years, we expect that electrical energy produced from nuclear power plants will continue to increase in the coming two decades, then start rising at an accelerated rate when we start approaching the second oil and gas decline phase, as discussed earlier (see Figure 19.0). I estimate that nuclear energy will represent, by the end of the oil and gas era, over 30% of the world's energy production.

With the foreseen post oil and gas shortages in other energy sources, (it is not expected that every country will have enough renewable and biofuel sources of energy at that time to replace fossil fuels), nuclear energy will be needed as a substitute. On the other hand, nuclear energy may be used to power large civilian ships, trains, and possibly planes. I strongly believe that the development of the miniature nuclear reactor will be a good and feasible technology, though it faces several major challenges. Some of the challenges that need to be addressed when considering nuclear energy is the handling of nuclear waste, safety, and security issues, besides the cost and availability of uranium in the case of large consumption of it by many countries.

5.22 Environmental Issues

As stated in the UN, Framing Sustainable Development Report (14) which is referred to The Brundtland Report – 20 Years On

"What is needed now is a new era of economic growth – growth that is forceful and at the same time socially and environmentally sustainable." Sustainable development – defined by the Brundtland Commission as development that meets the needs of the present without compromising the ability of future generations to meet their own needs. – Another quote from the same report:

"Current consumption and production levels are 25 percent higher than the earth's sustainable carrying capacity, according to the Ecological Footprint Sustainability Measure, an independent measure based on statistics. If everyone in the world were to live like an average person in the high-income countries, we would need 2.6 additional planets to support us all."

As per the Rio Declaration at the UN Conference on Environment and Development in Rio in January 1992, Agenda 21, the objectives of sustainable development are:
- Conserve the basic needs of life.
- Enable all people to achieve economic prosperity.
- Strive toward social justice.

Most studies, initiatives and reports about sustainability, stressed actions needed to meet above objectives, such as:
- The rate of consumption of renewable resources should be equal to or less than their regeneration rate.
- Input to our environment of all material and energy should be within the capacity of the environment to absorb them.
- Substituting renewable sources should exceed the consumption of non-renewable resources.

Furthermore, the world is facing challenges caused by air emission, pollution, all kinds of waste, including industrial waste. The oil and gas industry and its related industries have contributed significantly to these, whether through air emissions, liquid and solid wastes, or due to emissions from vehicles through the use of hydrocarbon fuels. With the massive introduction of renewable energy in the post oil and gas period to produce most of the needed electrical power, and much of this used to run many of our means of transportation, like cars, buses, and trains, it is estimated that the same will leave a positive impact on the environment, and will lead to the reduction of the carbon footprint.

Probably this will be one of the few positive aspects resulting from the absence of the oil and gas at that time. The new challenge relating to the environment, post oil and gas, will be from the increased usage of nuclear power, which if not done properly may cause some serious environmental and safety risks, especially if this technology is not regulated and controlled by reliable authorities, bearing in mind that the same may be deployed in new mobile systems, like ships, trains, and even airplanes.

The other big concern that we will have is the negative impact on the ecosystem due to deforestation, depleted water sources, and food shortages.

5.23 Biofuels and Biopolymers

There are many types and derivatives of biofuels. Biofuels, such as ethanol and biodiesel, are produced from conventional food crops, such as the starch, sugar and oil, that come from sources such as wheat, cane sugar, maize, palm oil, rapeseed, and corn. Biopolymers are produced from biofuels using certain processes. This market is growing, mainly in North America and Europe. Biopolymers have advantages over synthetic polymers, because they are environmentally friendly and they are renewable. Having said that, since biopolymers need land and water to grow, they will always have limitations on the volumes produced, competing with the food industry for land and water. Furthermore, there will be always the issue of production costs as compared to synthetic polymers. There is a major debate surrounding biofuels and biopolymers, in which some experts fear that a major switch to biofuels will create direct competition with the needs of the food industry, while others see no concern, as there are enormous areas of idle and abandoned land available. Production of one liter of biofuels requires about 30 square feet of land; this can barely drive a small car for 6 miles. This same land can be used to produce one kilogram of bread. This shows, in a simple way, the balance that will be needed to decide on the usage of water and land at the time. See how much land will be needed to provide fuel for millions of cars, each driving so many kilometers daily. All studies and research done worldwide on the impact of producing biofuels and biopolymers were based on current production rates and needs, and looked at the issue from a purely environmental point of view. As far as I know, none has examined the situation for the post oil and gas era, when millions of tons of biofuels and biopolymers will be needed on a daily basis to replace current fuels and synthetic plastics. The new situation is totally different and more serious. If we have to replace current fuels and plastics with biofuels and biopolymers, it means we will need millions of acres of land, plus huge amounts of water, which will certainly affect food production, and may affect the balance of earth's ecosystems. Today, with scarcity of water, the world will be striving to find new sources of water, while rationalizing the uses of existing ones. Similarly, we have issues on the availability of food; when, post oil and gas, there will be over 9 billion people on earth who need to be fed, the challenge will be enormous. The world needs to deal wisely with this challenge by having a balance between food needs, fuel needs, polymer needs, costs, and environmental issues; and at the same time, it must be looking for alternative products, energy sources, and means. Furthermore, new practices, technologies, and discipline will be needed when we use, produce and handle these scarce and valuable resources and products. Examples of areas of improvement and development that are related to using and producing water, include better and more efficient irrigation systems, water recycling and management, solar-based desalination plants, new breeds of genetically-designed plants that need less water, hydroponics (growing plants using less water), and aeroponics (growing plants in air).

5.24 Urban Planning

The new trends in energy production and distribution, and new challenges in people's movement, especially for long distances, are expected to drive societies into more distributed, autonomous, and smaller societies that are, to a greater extent, self-sufficient. Countries will delegate more authority to local municipalities; encourage them to produce what they consume; have their own medical, educational, and other services locally overseen, as much as is feasible, so there will be less need for transportation and movement. Local communities will produce their own power, which may be connected to the national grid. Movements on highways will decrease. Similarly, ports and airports will be less needed; hence, they will be re-designed to meet new requirements, which will involve the handling of either very large vessels and ships (driven by the new miniature nuclear engines) or small ferries and electrically driven ships and boats. They will have the facilities to handle respective cargo (estimated to decrease), provide power to charge batteries of electric engines, and provide maintenance services as needed. Similarly, airports will need to be designed to handle either very large super jumbo aircraft (driven by the future miniature nuclear engines) or small planes using electrically propelled engines, combined with solar power. Hospitals, hotels, schools, and other types of buildings and facilities will be smaller in size.

5.25 Education and Research

The post oil and gas era will mandate a change in the world education system, at all levels. Syllabuses, research, and educational material will have to be modified to suit the new situation. At the elementary levels, there will be a need to focus on creating disciplines related to energy conservation, which also should include an introduction to biofuels, biopolymers, renewable energy, electric vehicles, the importance of land and water, sustainability concepts, and environmental issues. At higher education levels, the same topics ought to be covered, but in more details, accompanied with more lab and practical work, site visits, and lectures by industrial experts. At the undergraduate levels, there will be major changes in several disciplines and degrees, such as:

- Chemical engineering: this will be significantly affected, as one of its main focuses is the downstream industry (such as refining, gas processing and petrochemicals industries) of the oil and gas industry, which will have shrunk substantially and changed to simpler processes, mostly related to biofuel production and biopolymers. In the interim phase, there will be a need to focus on other processes such as gas to liquid conversion, degassing of coal, and/or conversion of coal to liquids. The focus of this discipline may shift to processes and industries that will survive

the oil and gas death crisis such as biofuel processes, pharmaceutical, utilities, power plants, water systems and other chemical processes related to minerals.
- Petroleum engineering: as discussed above, this discipline will need to change to adapt to the post oil and gas era, where no or very limited exploration and production of oil and gas will exist. It has to shift focus to other types of industries, such as water exploration and extraction, mining, and so on.
- Electrical engineering: changes here would be limited to include more topics on renewable energy, fewer on conventional power generation (e.g., gas turbines, steam turbines) and new ways to transport and distribute energy.
- Computer Engineering and Computer science: focus will be in designing highly efficient circuits that need fewer plastics and less power; new types of materials and new types of operating systems and programs that can run efficiently on less powerful hardware. Furthermore, new types of computers will be covered such as quantum computers, biocomputers, and optical computers.
- Mechanical engineering: same as electrical engineering for the power side, plus more emphasis on new materials used to replace plastics, including respective manufacturing processes and equipment (e.g., metal forming).
- Architectural and interior design: the main shift here will be driven by the available materials at the time, whereas plastics usage will decrease against the increased usage of wood, aluminum, and other metals in building and decorating in new houses and buildings; beside depending on renewable energy to power homes and buildings by using features like roofs in the installation of solar panels.

Post graduate degrees and R&D programs, have to address new challenges and topics, such as renewable energy, new means of transportation, such as the Hyperloop, magnetic levitation, nuclear fusion technology, electric cars, electric ships, electric planes, new irrigation methods, genetic engineering in farming, new sources of fibers,

mining, rocket-like planes, new battery technologies, and miniature nuclear reactors. In the interim phase, the following need to be researched and improved:
- GTL plants[3]
- Coal gasification[4]
- Coal-based power plants

Furthermore, we should not ignore space-related research, where there are possibilities of developing new materials on the discovered planets, find new sources of energy, in addition to the remote feasibility at that time of inhabiting some of the nearby planets.

5.26 Petroleum Engineering

Oil and gas production is going to go through a tough phase when it comes to exploration and production of oil and gas, due to the need to address new, remote, and difficult areas and reservoirs, as well as the need to extract the most out of nearly depleted fields. It is expected that there will be a huge burden on the petroleum engineering community, in all its disciplines and specialties, to work diligently and smartly to try to delay the death of the oil and gas industry by using new technologies, methods, tools, and designs to cope with this unprecedented challenge.

---

[3] GTL plants: Gas to Liquid plants, it uses a refinery process to convert natural gas or other gaseous hydrocarbons into longer-chain hydrocarbons, such as gasoline or diesel fuel
[4] Coal gasification: the conversion of solid coal to synthetic natural gas or a gaseous mixture that can be burned as a fuel.

For example, petroleum engineers will continue to explore new, unconventional, and/or more difficult petroleum sources, such as:
- deep-water reservoirs
- shale gas and shale oil
- tar sand
- heavy fuel
- better and more effective reinjection methods
- extremely sour gas fields

They will also need to extend the useful life of each field of oil and gas to maximize recovery from existing fields plus finding new ones. This situation might need new tools and technologies, so as to produce more, while reducing the costs of production.

During the oil production decline phase, approaching the end of the oil and gas story, which is expected to happen within a few decades, petroleum engineers, and the entire world, will face additional challenges related to environmental impacts, earthquakes (there are claims that some of these unconventional production techniques contribute to earthquakes), costs of production, and so on.

The death of the oil and gas industry will cause the death of petroleum engineering entirely, in all its disciplines, or at least cause major changes in its focus, role, and responsibilities, such as a shift to mining, water exploration and production. Hence, we foresee major changes in respective petroleum engineering study degree programs (e.g., syllabuses, research focus, etc.). Some of the expertise used today in oil and gas exploration and production sectors may be used easily in other industries, such as drilling and geophysics services.

From the above, we will see before the end of oil and gas an intensive role and need for petroleum engineering disciplines, in order to delay its gloomy destiny, followed by either death of the discipline altogether or its evolution towards a new role.

5.27 The Food Industry

Today, even with the availability of oil and gas, the food industry faces challenges related to the anticipated shortage in food production, and the supply and availability of water. Environmental issues also are faced due to reduction in forestry areas. There are many countries that are facing hunger, drought or scarcity of water, especially in Africa. This situation is going to be worse in the post oil and gas era, caused by the need to use more land and water to produce biofuels and biopolymers. As explained previously, it is expected that production of these substances will increase substantially in the coming decades, to compensate for the loss of hydrocarbon fuels, such as kerosene, diesel, and heavy fuels. As explained in Section 5.28, the farming and agricultural industries need to improve and evolve, using new methods and technologies, for farming, plantation, harvesting, food production, storage, packaging and transportation. Using biopolymers

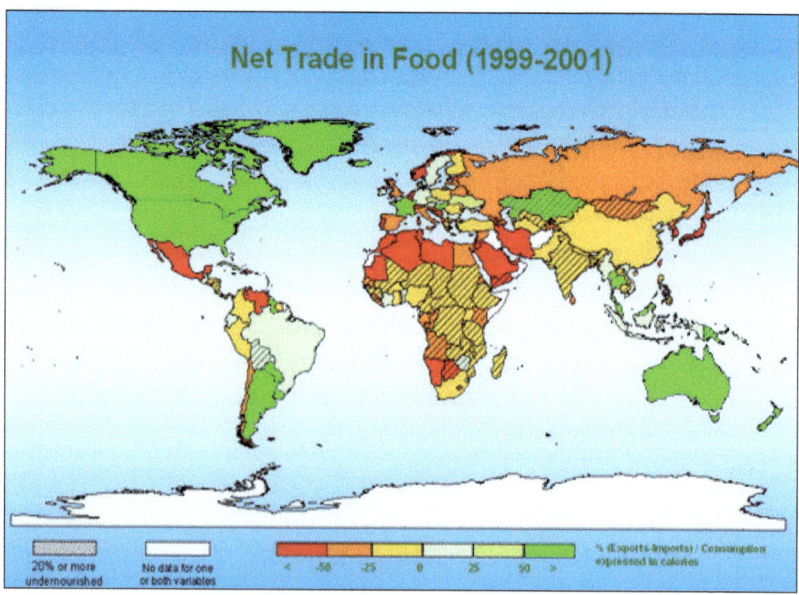

Figure 17.0 – World food trade map (15).

and paper-based packaging will increase. Also, and as discussed under Urban Planning and Transportation, it is expected that the world will evolve towards distributed and autonomous societies, with less need for transportation and distribution. Hence, most of these societies will produce locally and consume locally.

The map in Figure 17.0 shows the net world trade in food. As seen, there are few exporters of food in the world. Few in Europe are net exporters, such as France and Germany. It is scary to see many countries in Africa relying on food imports. Also, China and India are net importers of food; they have good agricultural output, but due to their huge populations they need to import some.

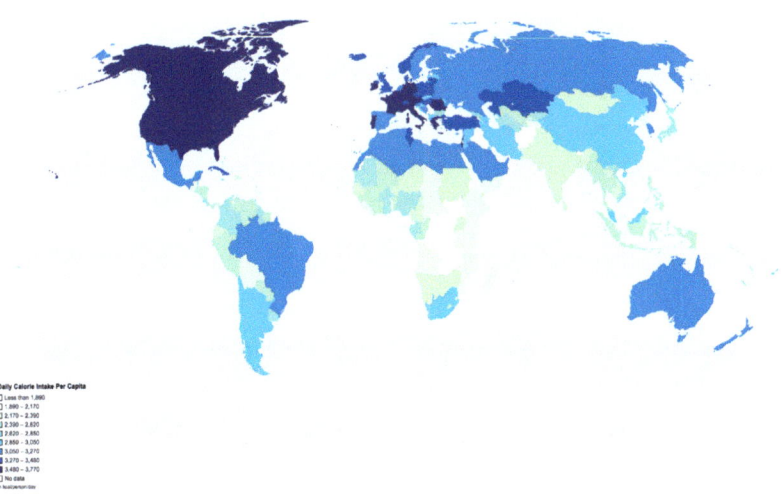

Figure 18.0 – Map of the world calorie intake by capita (16).

The intake of calories per capita per day varies from one country to another by a large amount. For instance, developed countries like Canada, the USA, and most of the nations in Europe consume much higher levels of calories compared to less developed and third world countries in Africa and Asia (18)(17).

It is obvious that the use of crops to produce biofuels will be at the expense of crops for food production. Crops used to fuel a car to drive for a few miles could be used to provide the daily food for one or more persons.

The FAO (Food & Agriculture Organisation) report from 2011(18) added; "The prevailing patterns of agricultural production need to be critically reviewed. A series of land and water systems now face the risk of progressive breakdown of their productive capacity under a combination of excessive demographic pressure and unsustainable agricultural practices. The physical limits to land and water availability, within these systems may be further exacerbated in places by external drivers, including climate change, competition with other sectors and socio-economic changes. These systems at risk warrant priority attention for remedial action, simply because there are no substitutes." They added that the world needs to face these challenges by taking certain measures, summarized by them as follows:

1 – the removal of distortions in the incentives framework, 2 – improvement of land tenure and access to resources, 3 – strengthened and more collaborative land and water institutions, 4 – efficient support services, including knowledge exchange, adaptive research, and rural finance, and 5 – better and more secured access to markets.

The report added; "Widespread adoption of sustainable land and water management practices will also require the global community to have the political will to put in place the financial and institutional support to encourage widespread adoption of responsible agricultural practices. The negative trend in national budgets and official development assistance allocated to land and water needs to be reversed. Possible new financing options include payments for environmental services (PES) and the carbon market. Finally, there is a need for much more effective integration of international policies and initiatives dealing with land and water management. Only by these changes can the world feed its citizens through a sustainable agriculture that produces within environmental limits."

The FAO report summarizes almost all concerns related to food production, consumption, and distribution among people of different countries, and land and water issues, as well as listing clearly all measures that are needed to face this challenge. Adding to these, the post oil and gas challenges that will be faced, makes for a gloomy outlook. On the other hand, if we take the FAO proposed measures besides the measures proposed in this book to face the post oil and gas situation then the foreseen challenges may be manageable by that time. As far as I know, all FAO reports, studies, and research, along with other food-related research done worldwide, have focused on the current situation without taking into consideration the additional impact of a post oil and gas situation. I wanted, therefore, to highlight the same and discuss this issue briefly in this book, hoping it would be an eye-opener for FAO and other specialized organizations to examine and include in their future studies and research potential post oil and gas impacts.

5.28 Farming and Agriculture

The farming industry is already suffering several challenges and shortcomings related to soil quality, water availability, insecticides, and pesticides for crops, along with other challenges; however, in the post oil and gas times, this sector will face additional obstacles, such as reduction in the available land for farming (assuming more land will be needed and taken to produce biofuels beside the impact of population growth by that time), availability of water, and availability of fertilizers (a major percentage of these come today from the oil and gas sector). Also, machinery used in this industry depends today on hydrocarbon fuels. The industry also is heavily dependent upon plastics for green houses, plastic sheets (to cover plants), and for packaging. Due to the reduction in the available land for food farming, it will be inevitable to maximize food production per piece of land per year using new technologies, such as geoponics[5], aquaponics[6], and petri dish[7].

In the absence of fertilizers, which are generated from byproducts (such as urea, sulfur, etc.) produced today from the oil and gas industry, there will be a need for alternative sources, such as products coming from biofuels (although these are expected to be limited, expensive, and not all practical), natural fertilizers, minerals such as sulfur, and/or other sources. There needs to be further research and development to be ready for the post oil and gas period.

The State of Land and Water Resources (SOLAW) report that was published by FAO (18), states:

"The world's cultivated area has grown by 12 percent over the last 50 years. The global irrigated area has doubled over the same period, accounting for most of the net increase in cultivated land. Meanwhile, agricultural production has grown between 2.5 and 3 times, thanks to significant increase in the yield of major crops."

This statement means that, with further development of new practices, techniques, tools, inventions, and rationalization, we can utilize existing land more efficiently to meet our needs. The big question would still remain; is the additional yield at the time, going to be enough to meet the increase in world's population and at the same time meet the world's requirements of biofuels?

Imagine the food and land situation when, post oil and gas, aggravated by the loss in fertilizers and plastics, and the impact of unavailable fuel on agricultural machinery, the situation is forecast to be serious. If we assume that agricultural machinery can rely easily on electric or solar energy or both combined, we still must ask: What we are going to do in the absence of a major source of fertilizers, pesticides and plastics?

---

5 geoponics: The science of agriculture.
6 aquaponics: refers to any system that combines conventional aquaculture (raising aquatic animals such as snails, fish, crayfish or prawns in tanks) with hydroponics (cultivating plants in water).
7 petri dish: Petri dishes are small, clear, plastic or glass containers that can also securely contain small animals or germinating seeds.

Competition for available land and water, which is already going to face additional pressure post oil and gas, in competing for water and land between production of food versus biofuels, biopolymers, cotton, and wood, will be made harder in the absence of critical items such as fertilizers and plastics and, overall, with the increase of population by an additional 20–25% by that time.

5.29 Sports

The sports industry will be affected in different aspects, depending on which sport and/or business. For instance, racing sports will be affected, due to the scarcity of petroleum-based fuels, which are used today in racing. Racing, therefore, may need to switch, either to electric cars (may be combined with solar-power and or biofuel) or to biofuel cars, or to a new rocket-type fuel, such as hydrogen. This will be decided based on extensive research and trials to evaluate both technical and economic feasibility. All in all, the impact will not be huge or critical for humanity. Sports like acrobatic flying will be affected much like auto racing. Other popular sports, like football (soccer), tennis, basketball, and swimming will be least influenced with respect to the game's rules, conduction, and proceedings. International events, such as the Olympics, World Football, International Tennis Grand Slams, and similar events will be affected, due to the foreseen travel difficulties, which will be slightly better than what they used to be eighty years ago, when aviation was not available as it is today and travel was limited to cars, trains, and ships. Hence, we expect that such events will have smaller live audiences compared to what they are today. Consequently, smaller stadiums will be needed. The other major impact on this industry will be related to the materials used to make sports gear, such as balls, rackets, golfing gear, boots, etc. Many of these, use one form or another of plastic or polymer. These will need to be switched to other products, or replaced with bio-polymer products if these are found economically feasible. Playgrounds using artificial grass or turf, which is based on some kind of plastics, will be avoided as much as possible due to its scarcity and hence high cost. Mobility of sports legends and stars will be limited as well. Movement of players, coaches, and referees between clubs in different countries, especially when these are far way, will be limited and less frequent compared to the situation today. Due to the reasons given above, the sports industry's revenues as a percentage of the world GDP, and their role in the world economy, will shrink. However, all in all, the impact on the world will not be critical.

5.30 The Space Industry

The space industry depends on rockets fueled by either solid fuel or liquid fuel, which are usually dependent on either hydrocarbon fuels or other fuels, such as hydrogen and oxygen or a mix of several fuels. Satellites and space labs use usually solar power. Beside fuels and the rocket engine needs, which are expected to be managed without oil- and gas-based fuels, this industry also uses components and items that depend on the oil and gas industry, such as plastics, insulation material, electronics, computers, and similar items. We also expect that the space industry will play important role in improving the land usage, monitoring, and control. Although the post oil and gas impact on the space industry is not foreseen to be critical, there will be a need to find suitable alternative sources and/or replacements for some of these essential items, especially the plastics-based ones.

I do not foresee that, by the early days of the post oil and gas period, humankind will be able to inhabit other planets, though attempts and work by many countries is being undertaken to explore some of these, notably Mars. Trying to be realistic, I expect that it will take a century or more for humanity to be able to live on one of these planets, though I am not sure that such an alternative will be economically feasible at that time, apart from being able to find noble and or new material on these planets that can form a good alternative to some of the diminishing material on earth.

5.31 Toys and Entertainment

Until the 50's and 60's of the 20th century, toys typically were made of a mix of wood, ceramic, leather, cloth, and metals. Later on, and with the invention of plastics, most toys started relying on plastics as the main element in their make. Today, it is almost impossible to find a toy without plastic, driven by its lower cost, light weight, ease with which to form and shape it and its vast availability. However, the new generations of children are becoming more and more attached to computer games and mobile apps, and it is expected that this trend will continue until the post oil and gas time. Therefore, due to the penetration of computerized games and the high cost of plastics at that time, the presence of conventional toys will continue to shrink and will be limited to young kids, infants, and babies below the age of 5. However, any remaining plastic toys will be expensive and used by the rich only because they will depend on biopolymers (plastics), or they will be made from alternative components, such as wood, cloth, leather, glass, metal or a mix.

Regarding entertainment parks and centers, where group games and equipment are offered, today many of these use plastics in their buildings, hence the same will have to be replaced by other non-plastic components, like wood, leather, glass, aluminum, or steel (e.g. swings, roller coasters, etc.).

5.32 Tourism and Hospitality Industries

The tourism industry will be one of the sectors that will be affected significantly by the absence of petroleum fuels, mainly for aviation and ships, including ferries and cruise ships. We may expect that other ground transportation means, such as cars, buses, and trains will not be affected significantly due to the use of other energy sources, such as electrical energy, hybrid sources (biofuels and electric engines), biofuels, and renewable energy, all of which are to a great extent developed and can be expected to be ready by that time. Global tourism relies heavily on air travel. Hence, the tourism and hospitality industry will be substantially affected if there is not a reasonable, affordable, and safe means of travel to replace the current form of air travel, especially for long distances. Some of the alternative means being examined are biofuel-based planes, which, though technically feasible, are not expected to be economically feasible due to limited quantities of biofuels at the time for all planes, plus associated costs. Fast trains are being considered and may be good alternatives, but for ground travel only. New technologies, such as the Hyperloop (if proven and available by that time) may be a good alternative, although it still needs a lot of research and funding to be proven technically and economically. Electric and hydrogen-fueled planes are also not proven and need to be developed to show that they are feasible at that scale, both technically and economically. Failing to have feasible alternatives to air travel will have a big negative impact on this industry, which may shrink significantly. Due to this impact, we can expect this industry to shift to more local and regional tourism, with reduced tourism at remote, far locations and faraway countries (as those need long-haul travel). Long-haul tourism will continue to be enjoyed by rich people who can afford the cost of biofuels, as well as supersonic and rocket-like planes. Such change will affect negatively many sectors and facilities that we are building and expanding today, such as airports, local transportation, food and restaurant businesses, retail, shopping, entertainment, exhibition spaces, sports, and many other industries. Cruises will be substantially affected and will be limited to the rich, unless, as discussed later in this book, we make the technology of miniature nuclear engines technically and commercially feasible for large cruise ships. The option of switching to coal or biofuel may not be feasible for cruise ships because of cost, pollution (in case of coal), and availability. Millions of people will either lose their jobs or switch to other businesses and industries. It is expected that we will need fewer hotels; these will become more local and smaller in size. In a nutshell, the tourism industry is expected to shrink.

6.0 GLOBAL IMPACTS

6.1 Impact on World Economies

As explained in the previous sections, almost every sector of industry and aspect of our lives will be affected in the post oil and gas era if we do not prepare, plan, and execute alternative means, energies, and solutions. The impact on world economies will take one of two scenarios; Scenario A: A smooth transition to new and alternative energies and means, as discussed previously. In this case, the impact on the world economy will be less severe, driven mainly by factors like:

- Impact on international trade between countries, due to difficulties faced in long-haul transportation. The degree of this will depend on how developed some of the alternative technologies are, such as miniature nuclear reactors, the Hyperloop, super-fast trains, etc.
- Absence of the petro-dollar (using the dollar as the only currency to buy and sell petroleum products), which will have a big impact on the American economy in the form of reducing its influence on the world economy, and resulting in a more balanced multi-currency world economy. Although this scenario may result initially in a big disruption to the US and the world economy due to the strong economic ties between major countries and the US (e.g., bonds, equities, trade, etc.), there should result a more stable and just economy afterwards. Such an impact might be reduced if proper measures are taken by all major countries during the transition period (phase II explained in Section 7.0) to reduce such dependence gradually.
- Control exercised by those countries that own and mandate new and alternative technologies, such as renewable energy, nuclear energy, new chemical processes, etc.
- Major roles for food producing countries.

- New and existing commodities that will play stronger roles in the new world economy, such as uranium, aluminum, glass, wood, and cotton.
- Roles and control by countries with advanced R&D, know-how, and technological advancements.

Some of the above may affect globalization adversely and result into more isolated economies.

Scenario B: Little or no cooperation, preparation, and planning. In this case, the world will face a serious decrease in energy sources. Although the decline in energy sources will take place gradually, it may lead to competition for the remaining fossil-fuel resources and, combined with short-term greed by governments and companies, with little or no orchestrated and global cooperation, could result in catastrophic consequences. This scenario will be expected to affect different countries at different levels and by different degrees, as follows:

- Countries that still have enough fossil-fuel sources, such as oil, gas, and/or coal that enable them to manage the impact for few more decades, assuming that they will not be subject to political challenges and threats by superpowers and neighboring countries that might need this scarce resource badly at the time. It is expected that during the ramp-down phase, that the prices of the fossil fuel and plastic commodities will rise sharply. There is also the possibility that industrial and developed countries, needing these commodities, may put pressure to exchange fossil fuel and plastics with important products and technologies that they control and own, such as nuclear energy, transportation means, renewable energy technology etc. This situation will cause major upsets to the world economy, due to the sharp rise in the price of certain commodities and impact on world trade.
- Developing countries that have nothing, neither fossil fuels, nor industrial or technology base, will face difficult times, hardship, and suffering. The people of those countries will be the main victims of the post oil and gas situation and are expected to face starvation, which may cause turmoil and increased illness,

combined with major migration campaigns to richer neighboring countries, which in turn could bring new problems to the world.
- Developed countries that have technology, large economies and manufacturing base. These shall play major controlling role, put their terms to others and try to trade what they have with what they need. Though serious conflicts may emerge at that level, between developed countries due to competition over land, resources and control, these countries are expected to be in better position compared to the other two categories described above.

I am inclined to call the post oil and gas time the "fifth industrial revolution," if handled wisely and smoothly, as discussed in the first scenario above, due to the foreseen major transformation in energy sources, technologies, world economies, and social impacts. Otherwise, it may lead to catastrophes, conflicts, and maybe to global wars. Overall, the changes brought by each one of the previous industrial revolutions were positive, as they brought new sources of energy, new commodities, technologies, and solutions. To an extent, each industrial revolution became a "spoiling" factor in a way, causing major complacency, driving huge increases in populations, and resulting in negligence when it came to using earth's resources, as well as instilling greed and fierce competition between businesses, which led, in many cases, to ill-manipulation of the world's resources for short-term gains. That is why I call the century, starting from the 1940's, the "illusive golden century," because most people, governments and businesses were deluded by the sudden growth in wealth, the easy money, the fast industrialization, and the higher standard of living. As per most studies undertaken in the past few decades, it is obvious that though some countries suffer from hunger, little water, and low standards of living, there exists in other countries huge waste of valuable world resources, such as energy, food, land, and water.

The post oil and gas era can either bring peace, development, a better environment, discipline, and responsible inhabitants; in this case, it is worth being called "the fifth industrial revolution," or it can bring destruction, damage, hunger, illnesses, and wars to the world, and in this case should be called "the third world war." Education, if directed, developed, and offered properly to all people worldwide, may help many in facing the coming challenges by preparing and engaging people as needed (e.g., birth control, doing things efficiently, conserving energy, improving productivity, etc.).

Overall, and in both cases, it is expected that world trade will shrink, growth will decrease, international businesses will be split or shrink and the US dollar will become an ordinary currency. The current stock markets will also shrink with no major centers, like London, New York, and Tokyo, these being replaced instead by many smaller local and regional ones. Countries that control technologies, such as nuclear energy (its technology and energy production from it), computers, electronics, biofuels technology, food, agricultural technologies, energy sources, and transportation means (technology and transport provision) will have stronger economies and will prevail.

6.2 Impact on World Trade and the Financial Sectors

The financial sector, post oil and gas, will be different from what it is today, mainly with respect to commodity trading, world trading volumes, and the main players in the markets. Today, oil and gas products and their derivatives are among the most important traded commodities in the markets. Some of these will just vanish, like crude oil, natural gas, and synthetic plastics, such as polyethylene and polypropylene. New commodities are expected to emerge, and existing ones (such as ethanol, methanol, biopolymers, aluminum, steel, wood, glass, sulfur, and food-related commodities) will become stronger, more important, and critical. Food commodities, although important today and heavily traded, will gain more ground and weight, and play major roles in the world financial markets, due to their high demand.

The major oil and gas players and companies will either disappear or change their business models by focusing on renewable energy, minerals, biofuels, and biopolymers. New players will emerge, especially those who started earlier in developing renewable energy technologies products or they have been in related renewable energy services. Countries that depend mainly on oil and gas will lose economic advantage, unless they start changing right away by diversifying their economies. World trade will shrink, become more localized, regional and isolated (rely heavily on ground transportation at that time). Similarly, stock markets will become smaller, local or regional. They will be less volatile and more predictable than they are today. At that time, the evolved social structure, which will be more distributed and localized, will result in an increased number of SME (Small & Medium Enterprises) companies, while large conglomerates, whose business model depend heavily on large supply chains and distribution networks, will shrink or disappear. Mergers and acquisitions may be another way at the time to modify and adjust the different business models of companies to cope with the challenges.

6.3 Geopolitics

With the scarcity of oil sources, especially during the transition phase, unless adequate mitigation plans, solutions, and alternatives are established on a fair basis for all countries and people, there might be serious geopolitical developments, wars and conflicts, much like what the world faced centuries ago. At that time, the invasions were to secure food, minerals, and other important resources and commodities, but this time it would be to secure access to the remaining conventional energy sources, fertile land, and water. As per all production, reserve, and consumption models for fossil fuels, there will be a huge unbalance in the distribution of energy reserves after 30–40 years, where most current energy resources will be depleted or close to depletion, while a few countries will be holding a relatively large percentage of the world's remaining reserves that will be needed by other countries, which are mostly powerful, industrialized, and advanced by today's standards. The fierce competition for energy in the absence of viable alternatives at the time may lead to serious political conflicts and clashes. Countries with diminishing or expensive energy may also face riots and unrest. New alliances and political or military pacts may emerge at that time to face these new challenges.

Countries that have nuclear energy knowledge and technology, and are advanced in developing alternative energy means and technologies will play an important role in the post oil and gas world. On the other hand, such technologies may be traded for the remaining oil and gas produced from oil- and gas-rich countries before the same is depleted. Similarly, countries with good farming, water, and agricultural capabilities and resources will be in better negotiating positions. The same logic applies to countries that are advanced in R&D, industrial ability, and technological skills, so they provide some of the new means, sources, and solutions for that period (e.g., the Hyperloop, high-speed trains, electric planes, etc.). They will be stronger in making their conditions and leading. With the spread and increased usage of nuclear energy there will be the risk of nuclear proliferation.

Consequently, I believe that there will be huge and bigger burdens on the UN in the coming few decades to lead, act as mentor, help, and put the world together to start planning and preparing for this phase, plus be involved in resolving new conflicts. Probably the UN needs at the time to be stronger and more influential, to be able to deal with the global and international challenges.

6.4 Military and Arms

Like other sectors, the military sector will be affected in various areas of business, mainly in relation to the material used to manufacture arms, weapons and other military equipment, such as plastics. The other impact will be related to fuel. Most military vehicles use diesel, some use gasoline, while planes use kerosene. Military gear and clothes will be affected as well, such as uniforms, hats, goggles, etc., which use plastics in their material. Like other sectors, electronics, computers, and electrical equipment will be affected as well.

The military drills and training will be affected and expected to decrease, especially when fuel is involved. Reliance on simulated and virtual training will be maximized. Due to the impact on planes and ships, most militaries will rely more on missiles, rockets, and onshore forces. Military ships and submarines, especially the large ones, will use nuclear power. Smaller ones may use a mix of solar and biofuels, and maybe the new miniature nuclear engines. Rocket-like planes are expected to be developed and proven by that time; hence, they may be used by militaries. These are fueled typically by other type of fuels, such as hydrogen or oxygen. More drone and unmanned tools will be used, all of which are solar powered.

6.5 Governments and Regulations

Due to the huge challenges faced in the post oil and gas era, and which in some cases are very critical, in the absence of proper mitigation plans, it will be mandatory for the world, including all countries, especially the powerful and advanced ones, to work together and cooperate, to develop collectively, suitable mitigation strategies, plans, and actions to face the post oil and gas challenges, which range from issues related to availability of food and water to transportation and other day to day needs. Failing to be ready by or before the absence of oil and gas may result in disasters, serious conflicts, and maybe wars. New international regulations will be needed, and existing ones need to be updated. There will be a need for a mechanism to ensure the duly and timely compliance by countries. UN bodies like the FAO and other organizations involved in overseeing the world's global issues related to food, agriculture, energy, the environment, and transportation need to play an important role to enhance cooperation, coordination, and collective efforts and compliance by all countries. Major countries, like the USA, Russia, China, Japan, India, UK and the EU must also work closely with the UN and play leading roles in such plans and initiatives.

Due to the foreseen decentralized nature of societies, it is expected that government bodies and their services will be decentralized as well. Besides regulations and collaboration, there will be a great need for discipline by people. Means of transportation that are essential for providing government services, including policing and security, will be given priority when it comes to consumption and distribution of scarce fuels, such as biofuels (in case solar or electric power are not suitable). It is foreseeable that local municipalities will also have major roles in managing local societies, bearing in mind that many of the centralized services today will be distributed and localized.

6.6 Impact on Selected Business Sectors

Table 1 – Summary of impact on selected businesses and sectors, post oil and gas.

SN	Business/Sector	Impact	Why?	Remarks
1	Mega projects, EPC contracting & associated services, subcontracting and services	Medium	Large percentage of current EPC jobs, especially large ones are done for the oil and gas industry; however, other industries, such as mining, power, and renewable, infrastructure will continue to need such services	Shift in focus; probably volume will continue to grow, after a short dip initially. Also, smart EPCs may shift during the transition phase to other sectors and industries by adjusting their model and using relevant experience they have.
2	Design, Manufacturing and supply of pressure vessels, static equipment and tanks	High	Most pressure vessels today are used in the oil, gas and petrochemical industries, with small percentage in power and other industries. New industries based on biofuels beside needs from the nuclear energy industry.	

SN	Business/Sector	Impact	Why?	Remarks
3	Process design and process licensing and technology	High	Major part of the process licensing and process design services are used in the oil, gas, petrochemical, and fertilizer industries; all these will be hit badly. New small processes related to biofuel, mining and fertilizers will continue to need them, but much less than what it is today	
4	Computer and electronics industry	Medium	This industry, though will continue to grow, it is going to be affected in two areas: • loss of oil and gas clients, which is minor, compared to the overall world volume and needs • microelectronics & manufacturing of Printed Circuit Boards (PCBs) whereby new material will be needed to compensate for the loss of plastics • lower turnover of computer and electronic devices driven by the longer cycle of usage, hence, smaller volumes of hardware, smarter system SW, plus "fit for need" approach. Also, high intensity computing, quantum computing, and new technologies will play important role in advancing the computing technology and industry. We foresee migration to more wireless-based solutions, so there will be less need for cables.	

SN	Business/Sector	Impact	Why?	Remarks
5	Asset Integrity Services, such as inspection services, non-destructive testing (NDA), in line inspection, pigging services, etc.	Medium	Such services are needed for any industry that has equipment, however the oil and gas is one of the main clients for it in the past few decades. This service will continue to be needed by other industries, such as mining, power, water, biofuels processes, transportation, etc.	
6	Aviation industry	High	This industry will be hit badly, including the manufacturing side of it, airports, services, and other associated industries and services. It will be limited to manufacturing small planes, smaller airports, and smaller service companies. Many related industries will also be hit badly.	
7	Tourism and travel industry	High	Tourism will be hit badly as well, due to impact on aviation and shipping. It will shrink and transform into a more regional and local industry. Associated services and industries such as travel offices, tourism companies, and other services, such as hospitality, will be affected.	

SN	Business/Sector	Impact	Why?	Remarks
8	Petroleum products storage and distribution	High	With the diminishing of oil and gas, there will be less need for storing and distributing petroleum products, such as gasoline, kerosene, and diesel fuel. These will be limited to smaller quantities and volumes of biofuels. Most petrol stations will switch to electric charging services, with a limited number of biofuel pumps.	
9	Hospitality industry	High	Due to the impact on the travel industry, all hospitality services will be affected negatively, caused by less international travel. The hospitality industry will be limited to regional and local clients. Many of the international hotels and restaurant chains will shrink and be replaced by local and regional operations.	

SN	Business/ Sector	Impact	Why?	Remarks
10	Power Generation and Distribution	High	Generation capacities will continue to grow; however, due to the major shift in the sources of energy, which will become more renewable (mostly solar), and some nuclear, the industry will shift to more local and regional power stations, fewer distribution networks (scarcity of cables), smaller plants, and fewer or no oil- and gas-based stations. Power plants, except for nuclear stations, will become simpler and easier to manage and maintain.	
11	Oil & Gas standardization, practice management and development	Medium	Many international standards, such as API, ASME, ISA, etc., were developed and built to serve the oil and gas industry; hence, they need to be significantly revised, to suit the new types of equipment, energies, plants, and services.	
12	Specialized oil and gas carriers (LNG, propane, etc.)	High	These carriers were built, especially to transport liquefied gas products, so they can be shipped long distances. Post oil and gas this service will not be needed except in very rare cases.	

SN	Business/Sector	Impact	Why?	Remarks
13	Shipping services	High	Shipping services as explained in Section 5.7, will be significantly affected. However, future shipping industry will be divided into three main categories: • small boats using mix of electric motors, solar and wind; • medium-sized ships using mix of biofuels, electric motors, solar, and wind, but designed to travel short to medium distances; • very large vessels and ships that use miniature nuclear engines, so can travel long distances to transport people and goods.	
14	Oil and gas machinery, rotating equipment, compressors, etc.	High	Such equipment will be less needed, since most of it was designed mainly for the oil and gas industry, except in the rare cases where these could be used for other services, such as air compressors, water pumps, etc.	

SN	Business/Sector	Impact	Why?	Remarks
15	Gas turbines	High	Will not be needed, as there will be no gas to drive them, plus most turbines at that time will be steam driven.	
16	Pipeline production, installation services	High	Most pipeline networks today are related to oil and gas, and mainly for gas distribution. Water networks are also important, however the pipelines related to oil and gas form over 50% (our estimate based on own experience and research) of the global installed pipelines.	
17	Valve manufacturing, design and supply (of all types)	Medium	Large percentages of valves produced today are used by the oil and gas sector; however, other industries still use valves and need them (e.g., water, power, chemicals, biofuels, etc.).	
18	Oil-related industries, such as E&P, refining, gas processing, chemical, and petrochemical industries.	High	These will all disappear or shrink vastly. Some may shift to smaller biofuel-based industries or biopolymer plants. However, all-in-all, these industries will be affected substantially.	

SN	Business/Sector	Impact	Why?	Remarks
19	Advanced automation services and solutions, such as Advanced Process Control (APC), Manufacturing Execution Systems (MES), and Refinery Information Systems (RIS)	High	Most of these services are used at oil and gas plants, and are unlikely to be justified for other types of industries, except simple systems and services for power plants, biofuel plants, pharmaceutical operations, etc.	
20	Shipbuilding	High	As per the Planet Energies report, dated July 2015, there are over 11,000 ships and carriers used for oil and gas transport; these form a major part of the worldwide carrier ships and vessels, so in the absence of oil and gas, this industry will be affected in both volume, size, and type of ships, as it will be driven by the number of ships produced and the type as stipulated by the energy available to propel the vessels. Most of the new ships will be smaller and used for shorter distances.	

SN	Business/ Sector	Impact	Why?	Remarks
21	Electrical equipment, cables, devices and other accessories (design, production and supply)	High	As explained in Section 5.0, due to the scarcity of plastics, there will be a need to design and produce this equipment using fewer plastics, and relying on new materials such as metal-based materials, paper, and rubber. Also, the trend will be towards overhead distribution systems and less on buried cables, so there will be less of a need for insulation.	

6.7 Social Impacts

The post oil and gas era will bring with it major social and cultural impacts. Today and for several decades, people became so dependent on oil-derived commodities, such as plastics and fuel, that the loss of some of these commodities will certainly have a major impact on them both as individuals and societies. As discussed in previous sections, the degree and effect of the change will depend greatly on how we handle the post oil impact. In case of a smooth transition, the social impact will be minimal and bearable, while in the other scenario, it is going to be serious and may be detrimental. In all cases, even in the smooth-transition scenario, people will have to change many of their current habits and lifestyles. Examples of these mean that they will have to:

- Give up things they use on a daily basis and switch to alternatives (e.g., natural fiber clothes)
- Give up or reduce imported foods
- Maximize usage of public transportation
- Live in smaller and decentralized societies
- Act responsibly when it comes to using water and energy
- Enjoy less tourism and travel especially to far countries and places
- Use home items, kitchenware, and furniture that all depend mostly on metal-based, wood, leather, and natural fiber items instead of plastics
- Emphasize a discipline of recycling plastics, food, textiles, and paper
- Rationalize the usage of paper-based products while at the office, home, or factories (e.g., stationery, toilet paper, kitchen paper, napkins, etc.)
- Produce and use what you need exactly; reduce and/or avoid waste.
- Surviving the consequential impacts will need more collaboration, both at the regional level and at global level as well

Societies, wherever they will survive the crisis, will become scattered, smaller, cooperative, and rely more on natural resources, producing most of what they need locally, armed with discipline, awareness, and responsibility. Societies and people will become closer to nature, appreciate it more, and be conscious of whatever new natural resources they will be having. In a nutshell, societies and people will become "closer to nature, smaller physically, bigger virtually, people more responsible, moderate, and aware".

I do not think it is worth discussing the pessimistic scenario, which if it prevailed, would bring chaos, hatred, greed, conflicts, riots, and probably wars; hence, it is not worth discussing the social transformation when people are hungry, at war, and facing death at every moment.

7.0 POST OIL & GAS: PHASES AND MITIGATION PLANNING

As explained earlier, the world is expected to go through three main phases before the end of the oil and gas era, as explained in Figure 19.0.

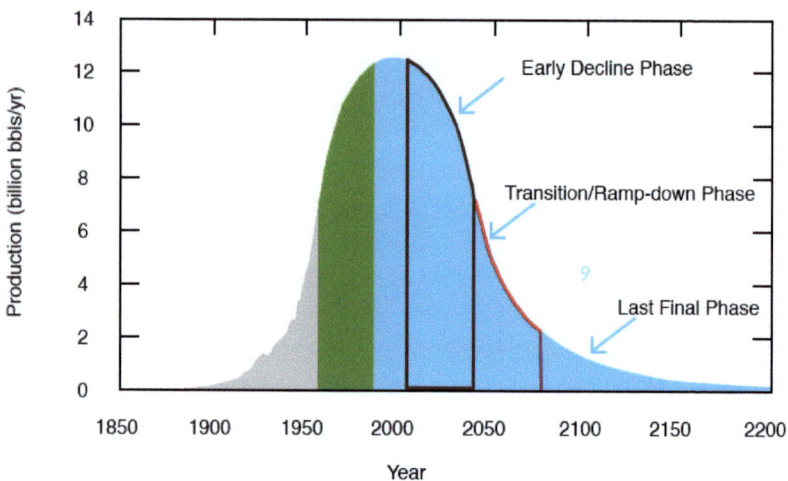

Figure 19.0 – Explains our definition of the ramp down phases, divided into three; early decline, ramp-down, and then the final death phase

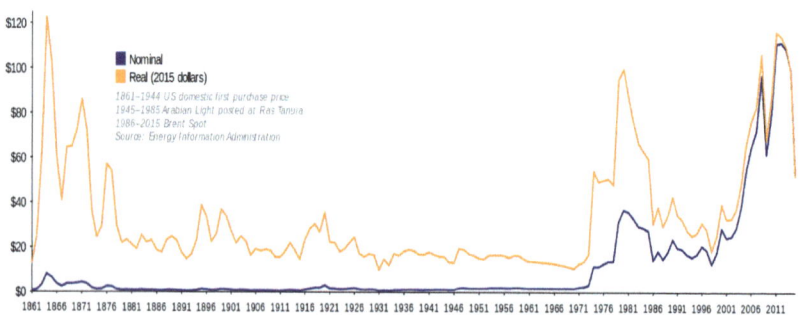

Figure 20.0 – Shows oil prices since it was discovered then adds our forecast for the ramp-down and oil depletion phases. (19)

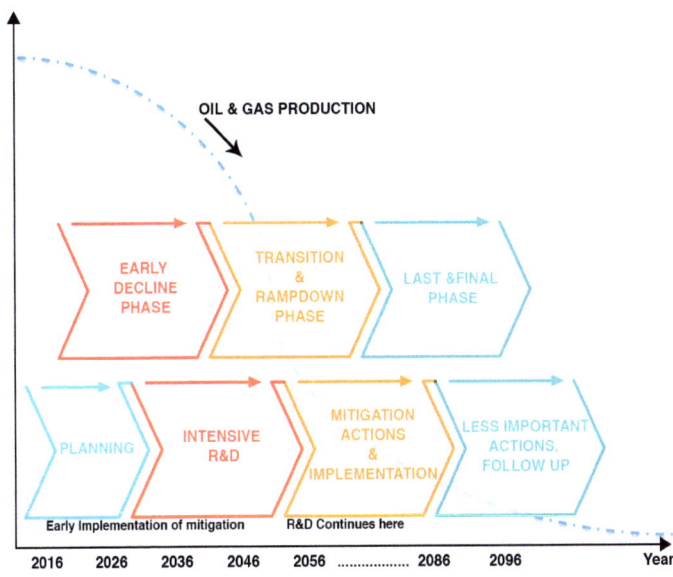

Figure 21.0 – Shows the proposed mitigation plan, mapped to the oil decline phases

Figure 21.0 shows the three main decline phases, mapped to the decline curve of the produced oil and gas, then against these the diagram shows the actions and mitigation plan phases proposed by me which are four main phases starting with planning followed by intensive R&D (to explore and develop new alternatives and solutions) followed by the implementation of the required actions (manufacture new technologies, alternative means, new sources of energy etc.) and the last phase includes the less important actions and research.

- Phase I – Planning & Preparation phase: This phase should start now and end in a few years, when suitable global management bodies, with clear and precise plans, have been formed, preparing for subsequent phases. In this phase, the world need to form a body or organization, probably led by the UN, supported by necessary expertise and financed by all countries, to lead and oversee the execution of these plans. In this phase, there is a need to put a plan together, which will include an extensive R&D program, besides a blueprint for all regulations, regulatory bodies, and new standards needed for the post oil and gas era. This body will initiate, guide, and lead a global, collaborative, and collective effort to prepare for the post oil and gas era. Such plans will be global, practical, collective, comprehensive, just, impartial, long-term (for at least 50 years), dynamic, futuristic, and isolated from the interests of the big companies, business lobbies, political interests, and local/regional interests. The roles will be agreed upon, defined, and distributed, so that every nation on earth has a role in executing this plan, depending on their capabilities. The leading team or committee will have the support of the best R&D centers and universities in the world and will work closely with them. This body will have the power to set priorities at all levels, so the entire world can focus on the main and critical challenges it is going to face, post oil and gas.

- Phase II – Intensive R&D phase: Starts when the execution of the above plan starts, and expected to last for 2–3 decades, when the last phase starts. The execution shall follow the set priorities, actions, and projects, as established by the above body and approved by different governments. The first part of this phase, will cover the ramp-down phase, before oil and gas are fully phased out. Hence, it will focus on better utilization of the remaining fossil fuels, followed by utilization of the remaining gas and coal, post crude oil (which is expected to finish before gas, then comes coal), by either generating liquids from gas, then generating gas from coal, etc., which may need specific research in these areas. In parallel, this phase will focus on optimizing the usage of the remaining fossil fuels. Furthermore, research will take place on alternative fuels, new sources of energy, new means of transport, new materials to replace plastics, beside other areas of research and development. In this phase, the focus will be on critical and essential needs, related to aviation, shipping, clothing, electronics, electrical systems, and food, using a mix of existing means, technologies, plus new technologies and means, developed for the permanent solutions in phase III.
- Phase III – Mitigation and implementation phase: This is the third phase and starts at the end of phase II, when there isn't enough

oil, gas and coal, and is expected to last for 2.0–2.5 decades. This phase will build on the R&D done in phase II, by developing the new solutions, technologies, and means, into practical and commercial products and systems, which can be deployed and extended to the public. By the end of this phase, the world should be, better prepared, to face the post oil and gas situation.
- Phase IV – Less critical actions-Last phase: This is the last phase which spans over the last 10-15 years of the decline curve and covers the less critical R&D and actions. This phase also establishes the foundation for continuous development and improvement plus for the future ongoing research and cooperation between the different countries on all fronts of knowledge exchange, joint research, trade, cooperation and so on.

8.0 LET'S GET READY: THE WAY FORWARD

In this section, we need to discuss and focus on priority actions and plans, which need the immediate attention of the world, due to the long lead time needed for research, innovation, development, testing, and implementation. These, in my opinion, are the most critical and essential to humanity; however complex; and call for investing huge funds; need time; and require collective, creative, and intensive efforts. Having said that, I am not claiming that what I am proposing or discussing here as areas of focus summarize all, or are complete, ultimate and indisputable. They are just the beginning to get the ball rolling, and to get others to join and initiate ideas, suggestions, and actions that can help the world.

8.1 High-Speed and Long-Haul Transportation

Although the world, as discussed in previous sections, will be seeking alternative fuels and sources of energy to compensate for the loss of fossil fuels, it might in some cases be able to find new means of transportation, mainly for long-haul heavy travel, like airborne and seaborne transportation, such as shipping and aviation.

Very few new ideas and technologies are being studied and examined, although there are a small number of ideas in the early stages of development that are, in my view, worth pursuing – if found technically and commercially feasible. Due to the high cost and complexity of some of these, adequate funding and R&D will be needed, and soon.

- The trans-Atlantic tunnel project, an idea for building a tunnel across the Atlantic Ocean, connecting Europe to North America, for mass transit; This idea envisages the use of advanced trains, or "bullets," running at very high speeds, reaching speeds of over 1000 km/hour. A few years ago, a new concept called the Hyperloop was proposed by SpaceX in the USA, which also started a global initiative to encourage people, teams, and countries to contribute to the same, with the objective for developing a full-fledged commercial means of transportation to replace aviation, ships, and the like when there is no fuel, post oil and gas (e.g., the trans-Atlantic tunnel solution). Similarly, it was announced recently that Scandinavian countries are considering building an under-water tunnel, connecting them together. There are numerous challenges facing such projects, such as the high costs, the time needed to build them, safety issues, health issues, design issues, etc. The aforementioned technology may go through two phases: Proof of Concept, so that once the technology is proven technically and commercially, it will first be used to transport goods only; followed by transporting people, once the concept is proven to be technically viable and safe.

- Recently, there was a demonstration in the UK of the world's biggest aircraft, which is a hybrid model, combining airship and airplane technologies in one model, using 1.3 million ft^3 of Helium to fly 48 passengers. Although this is in an early stage of testing, such a plane is doubtful to be an effective or feasible solution for long-haul, heavy travel. It may, however, be good for short-haul travel at lower speeds, and so cover domestic trips.
- Also, there are serious attempts in some countries to produce high-speed trains that are driven on an air cushion (aerotrains), and attempts to use solar power that is conveyed along the train tracks to power the trains, or in some cases a supply of hydrogen along the track provides energy for the train. These may solve some of the anticipated problems if they prove to be commercially and technically feasible. However, they will not address all of the challenges, especially when considering long-hauls across oceans.

8.2 Jet-Propulsion

Other ideas, propose using rocket-like planes, fueled by oxygen or hydrogen, or a mix of these two, much like space rockets. Such a solution may be good for high-speed small planes that can carry 3 to 10 people, and might be used by the wealthy and business people.

Some experiments and research already done in this direction, however, indicate that such systems need to be proven as technically and commercially feasible. Although this type of planes may appeal to some people, it may not be, in my opinion, of high priority for humanity.

8.3 Electric Planes

Figure 22.0 – Example of small electric propelled plane.

Electric planes, using a mix of charged batteries and combined with solar energy, might be a good solution for short-haul and light travel. It is easy to build propelled planes, which use electric motors, powered by sealed batteries, such as lithium-ion, and supplemented by additional charge (whenever possible) using solar panels installed on the body of the plane. However, due to the limited charge available on today's batteries and the limited charge available from the small area of solar panels, these will be feasible only under the following conditions:

- Light weight; hence, only a small number of passengers and goods can be carried by them
- Travel short distances before they need re-charging
- Need infrastructure at airports to deal with them (e.g., charge sources, maintenance, etc.)

The challenge in the case of electric planes (see Figure 23.0) is to create a balance between the weight of the plane, weight of the batteries and distance it can travel, while optimizing the cost. More charge is needed to carry more weight and travel longer distances. The more batteries you add, the heavier the plane will be, which may affect distances travelled plus put limitations on the carried-load. In my opinion, the main challenge for electric planes is to be able to produce batteries that have higher power densities and require much lower charge times. Although battery technology is being developed today at many research centers in the world, it is still far away from providing the solution for long-haul heavy travel by air. As per my calculations, there is a need to improve the battery power densities by at least a seventy times, and make the charge times much lower than today, so that we can start using electric planes for long haul and heavy travel. Such an achievement is far-fetched by today's standards; however, it may become feasible in a few decades. Also, new means for charging electric planes needs to be researched and developed (e.g. using laser beams to charge batteries remotely).

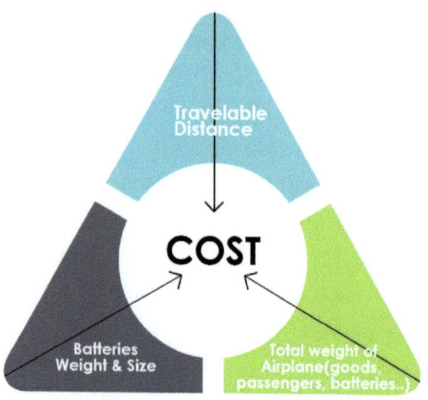

Figure 23.0 – Concept of the balanced design that will be needed for future electric planes.

8.4 Miniature Nuclear Reactors

The technology of Miniature Nuclear Engines is based on the Miniature Nuclear Reactor (MNR), which was studied during the very early stages of nuclear technology; however, it was shelved at the time for various reasons, such as security, safety, and cost. At that time, the main motives for considering MNRs, were to build small and modular power plants to replace small to medium-sized, coal-based power stations. In the past decade or so, research is progressing in several countries, like the USA, China, Russia, and the UK on MNRs or similar technology, for providing power for trains, ships, and even planes. An example of the same is the Small Modular Reactor (SMR) project in the USA. As most of us know, nuclear technology has been used in large military ships, ice breakers, and submarines for many decades. Though this seems complex and unfeasible for civilian applications, I believe it may be one of the good and needed "post oil and gas" technologies, especially for merchant ships. My argument is based on the following justifications:

- In certain types of transportation, like long haul loaded airborne and seaborne, there is limited research taking place worldwide, such as the Hyperloop, MNR, Hydrogen engines and electric engines.
- Nuclear reactor technology is proven, and has been used for a long time, including on ships, and works safely and successfully.
- The miniature nuclear reactors are not absolutely new.
- The MNR may be developed in such a way that it can fit easily on very large planes (several times the size of today's Airbus 380), and on very large ships, so it may be justified.

The challenges will revolve around issues related to safety, security, environmental concerns, and cost effectiveness. There also will be the challenge of uranium availability, especially if uranium starts to be used in a massive way. Based on rough calculations, I believe that if one MNR reactor can be supplied for 1 billion dollars or less, then these will be justified for large planes, ships, and trains. All that remains is the need for new regulations, security and safety measures, and new technical and aviation standards.

8.5 Biopolymers

Biopolymers are produced from living organisms and they are biodegradable. The materials used to produce them are renewable (as they are based on plant or animal products). Biopolymers are important today, mainly because of environmental issues; however, they will become more important, and, in fact, critical in the post oil and gas period, because of the absence of synthetic polymers at that time. Hence, biopolymers will become the only source of plastics. The challenge to producing them remains the availability of water, land, and the cost of production. R&D will focus on better utilization of land, water, and reducing their production costs. Yet it may be hard to compensate for all the produced quantities of synthetic plastics at the time, which is estimated today at over 320 million tons per annum worldwide. However, if we can determine the quantities of biopolymers required to meet the essential and critical needs (those that are not easy to do without) then we should be able to produce them (e.g., medical items, clothes, electronic items, etc.).

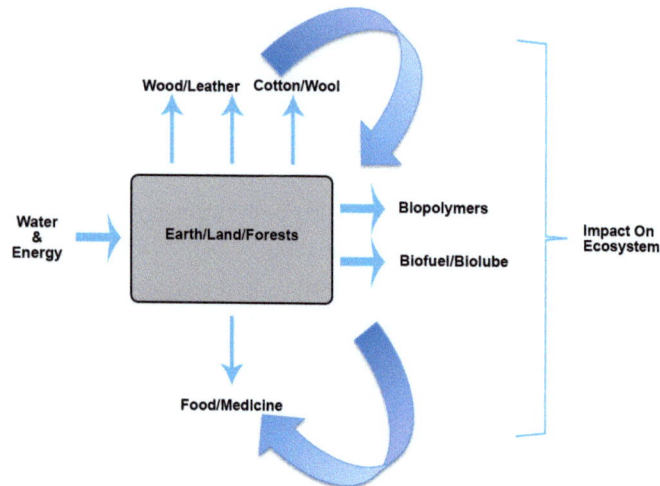

Figure 24.0 – The balance we need to keep, between producing biofuel/biopolymers, vs wood, food, water, and the overall impact on the ecosystem.

8.6 Alternative Fuels

One of the alternative fuels that have been subject to testing and research in the past two decades has been hydrogen. This fuel, when burned with oxygen, produces no emissions. It can be used also in a contained cell, such as an electrochemical cell, and for combustion in engines of vehicles. Similarly, it can be used in electrical equipment and cars. It can also be used in the propulsion engines of planes, as has been done in spacecraft and in liquid-propelled rockets.

The expected challenges are to be able to produce hydrogen in commercial quantities and at reasonable cost. Attempts are being made to produce it from seawater. There are established processes and technologies, to produce hydrogen, such as using electrolysis and the steam methane reforming process, which are widely used in the oil and gas industry. Today, there is research and attempts to generate electricity from wind, tidal or solar energy, and use it to produce the required electricity for the electrolysis process. Another challenge with hydrogen is the ability to store it under high pressure or refrigerate it and store it. Although it seems hard to use hydrogen widely and commercially, it is probably worth continuing current research, especially given the good progress that has been made with the respective technology that is already proven, so that all that remains to overcome are some challenges like finding optimized production processes, developing suitable storage, overcoming safety issues, etc. An area of feasible research and focus may be the use of hydrogen in boats, benefiting from the availability of seawater, to produce hydrogen during the journey.

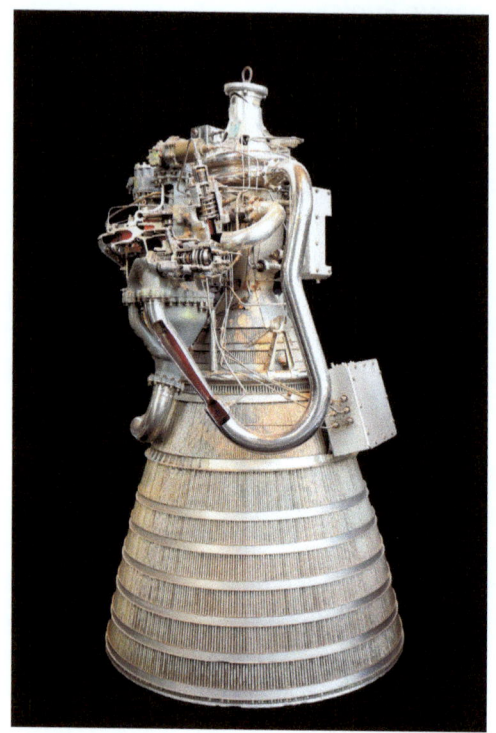

Figure 25.0 – Example of a hydrogen engine.

8.7 Electronics and Computers

With the fourth industrial revolution, the world became dependent on the computer and IT technology. Everything in our lives is becoming automated and computerized, so it became an integral part of our personal lives, societies, education, and work. The third IT platform includes the latest technologies forming the new platform for the latest computer and IT revolutions, such as Big Data, Social Networks,

Artificial Intelligence, Mobility and IoT[8]. Though the IT industry focus has been, in the past 30 years or so, on systems SW and applications, hardware will continue to be an important component of the IT world, being the holder and part of the system environment that any SW needs to exist and run. As our focus in this book is to study the impact of the absence of oil and gas on humanity, including the computer and IT industry, it forms an important element of our lives. In this section, we discuss priority areas of research and improvement needed to make the post oil and gas impact less harmful when it comes to IT, electronics, and computers. The same argument applies to other electronic devices, even if they use no software or applications. There are numerous electronic devices used by us on a daily basis, at home, at work, in transit. Based on my analysis and study, the main impact of post oil and gas will come from the absence or decreased availability of plastics, which are widely used in the IT and computer industry. The main areas of application of plastics are in enclosures/casings, on PCB boards, and on wires and cables used within those systems.

As discussed in previous sections, the world needs to find suitable solutions for these problems, so we may minimize or avoid disruptions, negative impacts or obstacles that may hamper progress and advancement of this vital industry. As discussed earlier, areas of research and actions for which to be ready will address alternatives and creative ways of doing things, such as:

- Longer hardware replacement cycles, supported by improved software and applications that are designed on the basis of "fit for need only" (FFN), so as to reduce the load of SW on the available hardware at the time, even if the same is of lower power and capability.
- Continue research on new types of computing platforms such as, biochemical computing and quantum computing.
- Study usage of alternative materials for plastics on PCBs and cables (e.g., copper buses, aluminum, glass, ceramics, etc.).

---

8 IoT: Internet of things, the interconnection via the Internet of computing devices embedded in everyday objects, enabling them to send and receive data.

- Use recycled plastics to produce additional quantities of plastics for this industry's needs.
- Use biopolymers only in limited and critical cases, where there is no easily feasible and cheaper alternative.
- Stop using plastics for casings/enclosures, and maximize using aluminum, steel, wood, and other materials as much as possible, saving any limited available plastics for PCB boards and electronic components.
- More wireless based products and solutions, so reduced need of cables.

8.8 Electrical Equipment, Cables, and Wires

Electrical cables, since the days of Edison, were made using all kinds of primitive insulation materials, such as ropes, paper, rubber, and so on. As seen in the figures, electrical cables have emerged and progressed since those days. Starting from the early 1940's, cable manufacturers started using plastics to make the insulation for cables. Similarly, other electrical equipment, such as motors, breakers, switchgear, distribution boards, and many others, began to rely heavily on plastics. Post oil and gas, plastics are not going to be available easily, and hence the electrical equipment and cables industry will be hit badly. They therefore will need to go back to more than 100 years ago, if there are no new suitable, reliable, and feasible alternatives available.

In this section, we need to discuss priority areas of research, where the world needs to focus and initiate R&D programs as soon as possible to find suitable alternatives for this industry. My initial analysis indicates that cables, breakers, and switches will be the main priority. The world needs to explore the feasibility of new options, although old methods for replacing plastics, such as paper, rubber, and so on, are also options. In the case of breakers and switches, cast metal casings and similar material may be used; likewise, ceramics can be substituted for other new materials. Considering the limitations, I see in using existing material, such as paper, rubber and the like, caused by the inferior specifications of these beside scarcity at the time and impact on our ecosystem, it is mandatory that we start looking for a new electric insulation material which does not affect earth resources, competitive in its cost, while meets our needs at the time. Not sure this is going to be an easy task, but worth exploring.

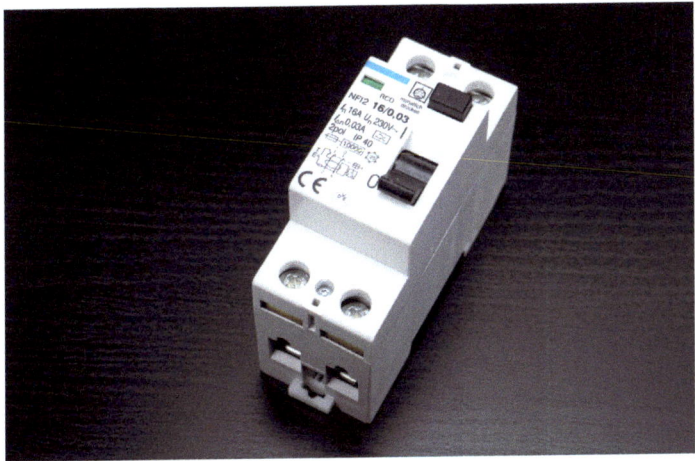

Figure 26.0 – Example of an old metal-based breaker, against the modern, plastic-based breaker.

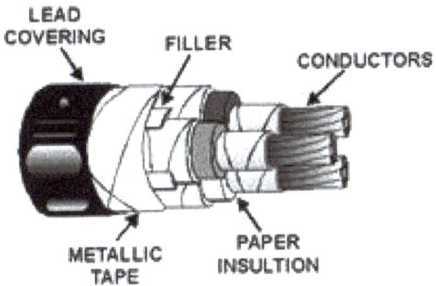

Figure 27 – Courtesy of the Naval Education and Training Professional Development Technology Center. Example of a paper insulated cable (20)

Design of electrical systems shall maximize using local electricity production centers, local distribution and use of overhead electricity lines (to reduce need for insulation) instead of buried cables.

The main challenges foreseen in this area are:
- Availability of enough plastics, whether from recycled synthetic plastics or from biopolymers, to meet the essential and critical needs of this industry.
- Competition with other industries and sectors that will also need such scarce materials at the time.
- Assuming we could justify going back to old methods of paper insulation, rubber insulation, and the like, with all their adversities, safety concerns, and the like, there will remain the challenge of not having enough materials of these types to meet the huge current and anticipated demand of the cable and electric equipment industry, which consumes today a large percentage of the world's plastics, estimated at around 5% of the plastic used today; this is equal to over 15 million tons every year (based on today's consumption).
- More paper will be used, which means more pulp, which is produced from wood, which means more trees need to be cut, logged, and used. This will have an impact on our ecosystem, bearing in mind that wood will be more and more in demand by different sectors, post oil and gas, (e.g., automotive, furniture, construction, etc.). This brings up again the need for maximizing the usage of recycled paper, to reduce the impact on our ecosystem.

8.9 Battery Technology

Batteries were invented a long time ago to store energy. Batteries are also called accumulators, as they accumulate and store energy. Another classification of batteries is based on whether these are vented or sealed. For the past decade or so, most of the rechargeable batteries used in the industry, at home, or in appliances have been sealed batteries. Sealed batteries are common and used in large numbers, compared to the early 1980's and 1990's, when vented batteries were prevalent. The main types of sealed batteries are, lead acid, nickel cadmium, and lithium ion.

In the 1990's, lead acid batteries were the leading sealed batteries for several years. However, lithium ion batteries have been gaining ground steadily since. In the past decade, they have become one of the most popular and widely used battery types in the world. They are used in cars, planes, computers, and mobile phones.

Batteries are also used within renewable energy systems, in UPS systems, and also in electric cars and vehicles. The world is becoming dependent on them in most alternative energy and new transportation means, therefore their performance is becoming critical for many applications and systems. In a post oil and gas era, the new alternative energy systems will become essential for humanity, and since these new systems will rely heavily on batteries, the world will need to put more effort and funding into related research for improving battery technologies. The main focus of battery research is addressing issues such as battery cycle durability, safety, power density, cost, recharge time, and robustness, as well as the impact of external factors, such as temperature cycles, high temperatures, and vibration. There have been several research programs to produce hydrogen peroxide from seawater, which can be used in batteries. There is also major research on new types of batteries, such as the lithium-ion flow battery, the lithium-silicone battery, the lithium-air battery, the sodium-ion battery, and research using nanotechnology in batteries.

It is estimated that the post oil and gas world will need tens of billions of batteries. The main challenge from now until that time will be

to improve battery performance and cost in several aspects. I believe that the critical aspects that need the main attention are:
- Power and energy density, hence weight per battery. This is critical when it comes to transportation means, especially when used in applications where the weight is an issue, as in aviation. Power density in certain cases like aviation needs to improve significantly, so that electric planes become feasible, especially for heavy, long-haul travel (see Figure 23.0).
- Consider installing standard and suitable battery charge posts at sea and land, on the main routes of ships, cars, and buses, that can be used to charge batteries over regular intervals (to be decided based on average and prevailing charge cycles at that time).
- Cost of batteries. This is important, bearing in mind the massive usage of batteries in almost all aspects of life. Hence, reducing their cost will reflect positively on the standard of living, on the feasibility of some new technologies, and on the overall world economy. I expect that batteries at that time will form a significant percentage of the cost of almost all services and commodities humanity will use at that time.
- Charging time. This is crucial when these are used to power electric engines of planes, cars, and ships, which need to be re-charged on a regular basis. Having non-feasible or unrealistic charging times, will render many of these systems and equipment impractical to use because of the long charge times. One option for handling this concern, in cases in which one could not reduce the charge time, would be to use a kind of "round-robin" arrangement for batteries. This would need regulations, agreements, and certain arrangements, i.e., low charge batteries would be swapped with charged batteries of the same type and capacity at the stations being used (e.g., airports, cars, ships.). This would call for a high level of international standardization of batteries with respect to types, sizes, charging systems, etc. This arrangement may increase the battery usage cost. Another option in case the recharge time of batteries remains high is to provide battery charge systems at homes and offices at an affordable cost.

- Robustness to stand external factors, such as environmental factors and vibration, so that a batteries' useful life is increased.
- Availability of certain materials that are needed to make the batteries, such as anodes, plastics, etc., some are today dependent on oil and gas products and others on scarce material such as Lithium and Cobalt.

8.10 Farming and Agriculture Research

As explained previously, there will be a need to change habits, practices, and cultures of people, so that we rationalize out usage of food, water, and energy. Furthermore, recycling of food, like recycling of other scarce commodities at the time, will be crucial for humanity. Research needs to focus on so many important areas for improving the farming and agricultural technologies. Example of areas of improvement and development are new and effective ways of producing water, more efficient irrigation systems, water recycling and management, solar-based desalination plants, new breeds of genetically designed plants which need less water, besides using other technologies, such as, hydroponics (which uses less water), and aeroponics (growing plants in air). Areas of research and improvement will try to achieve the following guidelines and objectives:

- obtain higher yield of crop production from same area of land;
- gain less usage and or need of water for the same amount of production;
- recycle as much as is feasible (recycled food can be used as fertilizer, or to feed animals, etc.);
- find new ways of growing plants (e.g., in water, in oceans, in air, in space, etc.);
- find new substitutes for pesticides, insecticides, and fertilizer, to those obtained today from oil and gas.

- rationalize consumption of food and water by people
- collaborate at international level between all countries to achieve an acceptable intake per capita of food and water, irrespective of where this person is living

8.11 Recycling

As discussed earlier in several sections, there will be a great need for recycling in almost all aspects of human life, right from recycling of paper, wood, cotton, wool, food and many others. At the time, the main driver for recycling will not be environmental issues and concerns, which are genuine and important, but life necessities and needs. Hence, it will be important that the world starts by developing new recycling technologies, encourage collection and storing of these important recyclable items right from today, developing reliable methods for storing these, and creating the right level of awareness and discipline towards recycling, especially in less developed countries. Recycling will be so crucial to human life at that time, supporting our day-to-day needs plus driving our economy, therefore, the world economy then, as I want to describe it, will be called **"the recycled economy"**.

9.0 SUMMARY AND CONCLUSION

I did not find a better diagram than Figure 28.0 to summarize, the issues, solutions, concerns and impacts, all on one page, so that a normal reader can grasp the essence of this book, which is addressing the situation of the world in the post oil and gas era.

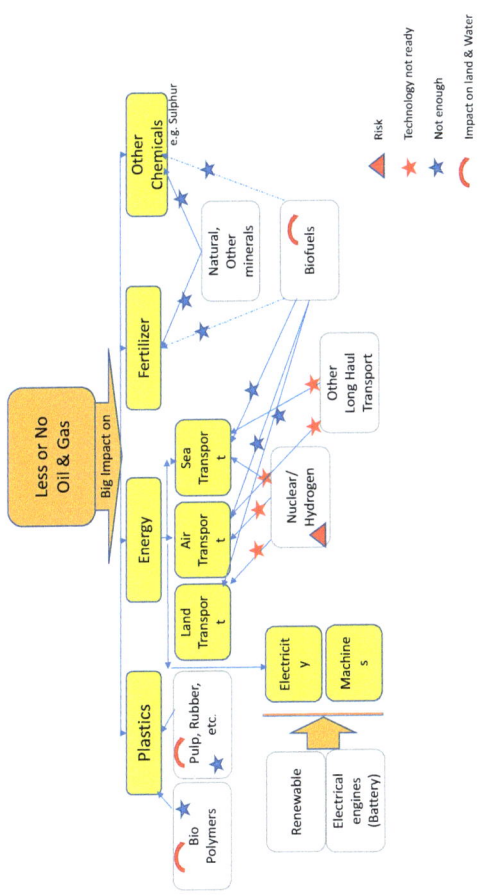

Figure 28.0 – Shows a summary of the main utilizations of fossil fuels today and possible alternative, the level of development of each alternative and associated risks of each.

This diagram summarizes the impacts caused by the absence or the decreased availability of oil and gas on different aspects of our lives. It also shows the main alternatives for each case, classified as either "not enough," "not developed," or has "other risks" associated with it. It also shows if that alternative may have an impact on the earth's ecosystem,

The figure above uses the Cause & Effect principle to explain in a simple and graphical way the main impacts on the world, post oil and gas, and the possible solution and alternatives for each:

- Production of energy: Oil and gas have been the main source of energy for humanity for almost 100 years or so, mainly for producing electricity and for transportation, besides other less important services, such as to provide fuel for machinery, domestic heat and others applications. The first one, generating electricity and supplying it to people, factories, etc. Although this application of oil and gas is crucial, huge, and very important for humanity, I am less concerned here, because the world have proven to have well-developed and affordable alternatives, being primarily nuclear and renewable energy (mainly wind and solar). Although, today, these are not used on a wider scale compared to fossil fuels, I believe that with the decreasing cost of these alternatives, they will prevail for producing electricity and support some of the means of transportation, provided we put in place the right, accelerated global plans and follow them.

The other service, as explained in the diagram, is land transport, including trains, cars, buses, trucks, etc.

Again, I am not worried about it. We will have electric cars, hybrid cars, some with biofuel (which will be limited due to scarcity and cost), probably some trains may use some kind of nuclear energy, as discussed earlier.

The main challenge, as discussed in previous chapters and explained in the diagram, will be "long-haul transportation," this being airborne and seaborne. To handle this huge challenge, which is very essential for the survival and development of the civilized world and humanity, we need a suitable alternative energy or means for replacing oil and gas. In previous chapters, we discussed several options, as explained, apart from biofuel, which unfortunately is not going to be plentiful enough to serve all the world's needs, due to scarcity and competition with food on land and water, and although technically developed, it is not considered an adequate and feasible resource to fuel all seaborne and airborne means of transportation at the time, which will need huge amounts of fuel. Other means or alternative energy sources, like miniature nuclear engines, and Hyperloops, may prove feasible as good technical alternatives, but being new and not fully developed, may take time to prove and develop, plus prove their feasibility.

It is hard to see the world without adequate seaborne and airborne means of transportation, especially for long distances, hauling heavy loads. As explained earlier in the book, there are going to be feasible (at least technically) alternatives, using a mix of electric engines, solar, wind, etc. for short-haul and light seaborne and airborne transportation.

As explained in the diagram, there is another major impact and big concern for humanity: plastics. As explained earlier in the book, there isn't a ready alternative for plastics today. Some alternatives, although proven, will not be enough, like biopolymers, pulp and paper, rubber, cotton, etc. Needless to mention, there is the impact on our ecosystem, the competition for land, food, etc. Therefore, I strongly believe that this area needs utmost attention, extensive R&D, proper planning and preparation, so we can find feasible alternatives, both technically and commercially, without jeopardizing our environment, ecosystem and food resources.

The other two areas that have impact are producing fertilizers and other chemical products. The main challenges here is to make sure that the alternatives sought, as most likely they will be natural minerals, such as phosphates, sulfur, etc., can be produced in the needed quantities for a long time, since there will be a need to produce them in larger quantities at the time.

Table 2.0 is a Summary of the main candidate alternative sources of energy & relevant commodities, with indications of the development status and suitability of each, along with associated risks, and their impact on the earth's ecosystem, if any, (the overall balance of our ecosystem, and not only pollution and emissions concerns).

SN	Alternative	Feasible Technically	Feasible Commercially	Adequate and Enough	Risks Involved	Effects on Eco system	Have Concern?
1	Renewable Energy to produce electricity	Yes	Yes	Yes	None	None	No
2	Electrical energy (connected or using batteries) for land transportation	Yes	Yes, though in case of batteries more R&D needed to extend their life, reduce cost and weight	Yes	Acceptable and not higher than what we have today from fuel driven vehicles	None	No
3	Electrical Energy for airborne travel (may be combined with renewable)	Still experimental, limited to small planes but not for heavy, long-haul planes	Still expensive even for small ones	Not yet, even for small planes	Acceptable, if proven	None	Yes, Big concern

SN	Alternative	Feasible Technically	Feasible Commercially	Adequate and Enough	Risks Involved	Effects on Eco system	Have Concern?
4	Electrical Energy for seaborne travel (mix with solar and wind)	Electric engines are not new and were proven on ships long time ago, however for large ships and travel of long distances, this is not proven yet, may be feasible for small boats and ships	Once proven technically, cost to build should be comparable with current ships; operating cost should be lower than current boats/ships. Electric engines should be simpler and easier to build, compared to current engines	If proven for small ships; need time to meet market requirement of large number of ships	Acceptable if proven	None	Yes, Big concern
5	Nuclear to produce electricity	Yes, for many years	Yes, over the age of the power plant	Yes	Yes, however could be mitigated with the right design, material and construction	Possible because of nuclear waste	Possible however if necessary measures are taken these concerns will be less

SN	Alternative	Feasible Technically	Feasible Commercially	Adequate and Enough	Risks Involved	Effects on Eco system	Have Concern?
6	Nuclear for airborne	Not yet, some early R&D. If successful, could be feasible for very large super jumbos to justify the cost (2000 passengers and above)	to be checked	If proven, needs time to develop and produce	Yes, need to be studied carefully (accidents, pollution, hijacking, etc.)	See above	Yes,
7	Nuclear for seaborne	Proven for some military ships and submarines, however still needs more R&D to be used for commercial use. Most likely will be feasible for very large vessels to justify the high cost e.g. super cargo vessels, large cruise ships etc.	to be checked	If proven; needs time to produce	Same as above	See above	Somewhat, however more feasible than aviation

SN	Alternative	Feasible Technically	Feasible Commercially	Adequate and Enough	Risks Involved	Effects on Eco system	Have Concern?
8	Nuclear for trains	Early stages of research, by some countries, yet to be proven	To be checked against cost of current engines and savings in electricity cost	Needs time to produce once proven	Same as above	see above	Like ships though easier to protect and justify
9	Biofuel for land travel	Yes, proven	Expensive than conventional fuel. Prices may go higher if there is higher demand for biofuels	Not really, even if we manage to use most of the available land on earth, will not be enough to meet the world fuel demands. Also will be at the expense of food and water	None	None, unless we remove forests for biomass, etc., then it will	Yes, because of impact on land, water and eco-system
10	Biofuel for airborne	Yes, proven though not at very large scale	Same as above	Same as above	None	Same as above	Same as above

SN	Alternative	Feasible Technically	Feasible Commercially	Adequate and Enough	Risks Involved	Effects on Eco system	Have Concern?
11	Biofuel for seaborne	Not tried like airborne and land travel, however should be easy to prove on ships	Same as above	Same as above	None	Same as above	Same as above
12	Biopolymers for plastics	Yes, proven technology	More expensive and expected to skyrocket in price, when synthetic plastics start decreasing	Not sure there will be enough quantities	None	Same as above	Quantities not enough plus competes for land and water with food
13	Paper and Rubber replace plastics	Can replace for some usages, such as cable insulation, bags, plastic films, furniture etc.	Expected to be slightly more expensive, yet to be checked	Availability of these today is limited, increasing their production will affect food and water availability	None	Same as above, these products need more land and water	Volumes limited plus impact on ecosystem, competes with food and for land and water

SN	Alternative	Feasible Technically	Feasible Commercially	Adequate and Enough	Risks Involved	Effects on Eco system	Have Concern?
14	Wood, cotton, wool, glass, replace plastics	Same as above	Same as above	Same as above	None	Same as above	Same as above plus not sure we can meet the volume requirements
15	Minerals replace oil & gas products, e.g., sulfur, etc.	Proven but available quantities need to be checked, and for how many years	Expected to be slightly more expensive	Yet to be checked, especially if quantities needed are big	None	Possible to be checked	Somewhat, need to check available reserves
16	Natural and minerals replace urea and ammonia	Same as above	Same as above	Same as above	None	Same as above	Same as above
17	Use of metals to replace plastics for some applications e.g., aluminum, steel, etc., in furniture, doors, windows, cars	Yes, if enough quantities available	May be slightly more expensive	To be checked	None	Same as above	Same as above

Table 2.0 – Summary and analysis of the main candidate alternatives of energy sources and commodities.

The above discussion, the summary table, and diagram should lead us to the following conclusion of this book:

The world is not yet ready for the "Post Oil & Gas era." If some of us have the illusion that we have ready alternatives for all of the problems, so that there is no bother, then we are deceiving ourselves and putting our children and grandchildren in great jeopardy, because of our ignorance, greed, and complacency. Those, the "thought-to-be ready" alternatives, need extensive research and development before we can say we are ready or not, because they are either not enough (quantity wise), affect our ecosystem, affect our food supply, are expensive, are not well-developed technically, are risky, or are some of these combined.

Therefore, if we DO NOT MOVE NOW, COLLECTIVELY, SERIOUSLY, guided by one Global Strategy and Plan, away from politics, greed, and business interests, then HUMANKIND IS GOING TO SEE ITS WORST DAYS BEFORE THE END OF THE CENTURY.

As Napoleon Said; "Gouverner, Cest Prevoir" meaning, "to manage is to forecast."

REFERENCES

(1) British Petroleum.(2016)*BP Statistical Review of World Energy June 2016*
(2) Energy Information Administration.(2013)*Technically Recoverable Shale Oil & Shale Gas Resources: An Assessment of 137 Shale Formalities in 41 Countries Outside the United States June 2013*, Retrieved from www.eia.gov/analysis/studies/worldshalegas/pdf/overview.pdf
(3) Canada Association of Petroleum Producers.(2017) Retrieved from www.capp.ca/canadian-oil-and-natural-gas/oil-sands/oil-sands-development
(4) Paul Chefurka, Retrieved from http://www.paulchefurka.ca/Population.html
(5) Rocky Mountain Institute ©. (2011) *Reinventing Fire*. Published by Chelsea Green. Retrieved from https://rmi.org/insights/reinventing-fire
(6) M. King Hubbert. (1971*) Energy and Power A Scientific American Book.*
(7) Sfoucher. (2008). Retrieved from https://en.wikipedia.org/wiki/File:Hubbert_US_high.svg Copyright © & M. King Hubbert. (1955) *Nuclear Energy and the Fossil Fuels. Published in Drilling and Production Practice.* American Petroleum Institute.
(8) Energy Information Administration. *World Oil Production, 1900 – 2009* and US Census Bureau International Data Base. *World Population 1000 AD – 2010AD*. Exact graph taken from: www.peterevansphotography.co.nz/writing/zealandia.html
(9) Gail Tyerberg. (March 12,2012) *World energy Consumption 1820 in Charts*. Retrieved from https://ourfiniteworld.com/2012/03/12/world-energy-consumption-since-1820-in-charts/
(10) Energy Information Administration.(2016) *International Energy Outlook , July 2016*.Retreived from www.eia.gov/outlooks/ieo/pdf/0484(2016).pdf
(11) Michael McDonald. (July 23,2015)*What Miniature Nuclear Reactors Could Mean For The World*. Retrieved from http://oilprice.com/Alternative-Energy/Nuclear-Power/What-Miniature-Nuclear-Reactors-Could-Mean-For-The-World.html

(12) Royal Society of Chemistry.(2014) *Bi- and tri-dentate imino-based iron and cobalt pre-catalysts for ethylene oligo-/polymerization*, *Inorganic Chemistry Frontiers*,. Retrieved from http://pubs.rsc.org/en/content/articlelanding/2014/qi/c3qi00028a#!divAbstract

(13) World Bank.(2013) *World Development Indicators*. Retrieved from http://wdi.worldbank.org/table/3.7

(14) United Nations. (1987)*Our Common Future, Chapter 2: Towards Sustainable Development: Report of the World Commission on Environment and Development* Retrieved from A/42/427. www.un-documents.net/wced-ocf.htm

(15) Food and Agriculture Organization of the United Nations.(2003) *FAOSTAT. Net trade in food(dataset)*.Retrieved from http://faostat.fao.org/Portals/_Faostat/documents/pdf/map05.pdf

(16) ChartsBin statistics collector team 2011, *Daily Calorie Intake Per Capita*, ChartsBin.com, viewed 30th May, 2017, http://chartsbin.com/view/1150

(17) Daily Mail Online. (August 12,2014) *Daily Calorie intake of countries across the world revealed… and (surprise) the U.S. tops the list at 3,770*, by Margot Peppers for Mailonline. Retrieved from www.dailymail.co.uk/femail/article-2722815/Daily-calorie-intake-countries-world-revealed-surprise-U-S-tops-list-3-770.html

(18) Food and Agriculture Organization of the United Nations and Earthscan. (2011) *The state of the world's land and water resources for food and agriculture. Managing systems at risk*

(19) Tomthehand (2008). Retrieved from https://commons.wikimedia.org/wiki/File:Oil_Prices_Since_1861.svg updated by Delphi234 Copyright ©

(20) Naval Education and Training Professional Development and Technology Center. Manual. Retrieved from www.rfcafe.com/references/electrical/NEETS-Modules/images/04111img68.gif

(21) Plastic Insight, plasticinsight.com

INDEX

page 21: © Paul Chefurka
page 22: © Rocky Mountain Institute
page 23: © M. King Hubbert. (1971) Energy and Power, A Scientific American Book
page 23: © Wikipedia
page 24: © www.peterevansphotography.co.nz
page 27: © Gail Tyerberg
page 28: © EIA, International Energy Outlook, July 2016
page 40: © Royal Society of Chemistry
page 41: © Shutterstock
page 44: © Pixabay
page 44: © Shutterstock
page 46: © 123RF Technology Limited
page 47: © 123RF Technology Limited
page 49: © Pixabay
page 51: © Shutterstock
page 52: © 123RF Technology Limited
page 70: © FAO
page 71: © chartsbin
page 98: © Dr. Issam Wadi
page 98: © Wikipedia
page 99: © Dr. Issam Wadi
page 104: © Wikipedia
page 106: © Dr. Issam Wadi
page 108: © Dr. Issam Wadi
page 110: © Shutterstock
page 113: © Pixabay/inspectapedia
page 113: © Naval Education and Training Professional Development and Technology Center.
page 119: © Dr. Issam Wadi

The author

With over forty years in the Oil and Gas industry, Dr Wadi is an authority in the field with a focus on research, engineering and design of oil and gas plants and systems. He was involved in major oil and gas projects, studies, consultancies and initiatives, all around the world. He has special interests in the application of advanced technology into the energy industry to improve performance and economics.

Dr. Wadi became a regular speaker at many international oil, gas and relevant technology conferences. Dr Wadi has special research interests in the area of Advanced Automation, Artificial Intelligence Applications, Optimization and Performance Management in the energy industry.

He is a guest lecturer at some UK universities and has seen several of his articles published in international journals.

novum PUBLISHER FOR NEW AUTHORS

The publisher

He who stops getting better stops being good.

This is the motto of novum publishing, and our focus is on finding new manuscripts, publishing them and offering long-term support to the authors.
Our publishing house was founded in 1997, and since then it has become THE expert for new authors and has won numerous awards.

Our editorial team will peruse each manuscript within a few weeks free of charge and without obligation.

You will find more information about
novum publishing and our books on the internet:

www.novum-publishing.co.uk